2000
P

AMERICAN PROTESTANTISM:

An Appraisal

AMERICAN PROTESTANTISM:

An Appraisal

by

T. Valentine Parker

PHILOSOPHICAL LIBRARY

New York

TABLE OF CONTENTS

PREFACE

The purpose of the following chapters is to appraise American Protestantism. Unfortunately many of the people of our churches do not know what Protestantism is. Many of the leaders are so busy getting things done that they have not the leisure to try to put together the many inconsistent elements of Protestantism to form a picture of the whole let alone to discover the excellencies and defects of the picture. And in our day there is so much in our churches pressing for very thoughtful consideration and decision that attempts should be made to present such an appraisal as we are attempting here.

The introductory chapter, different as it is from the other chapters, is inserted not only for the benefit of those who need to have their memories refreshed concerning the history of the church and the origin of Protestant churches, but because the pertinence and significance of the subsequent discussion are brought into focus by a consideration of historical backgrounds and their logical implications. The chapter makes no pretension to historical research or to a rewriting of history.

The subsequent chapters of necessity reiterate much that has already been written. This is especially true of the chapter under the caption "The Church Glorious." Many of the defects of the church have also and often been enumerated, but in general this has been in piecemeal fashion and without an appraisal of their effects upon the fundamental values of the church. The attempt is made in these pages to do that very thing. The Christian minister is so concerned with his multitudinous duties that he has a tendency to evade the implications that are in the conception of the ministry and the so-called "layman" has only a casual perception of what the ministry is. These days many books have been written on worship, but they have all more or less followed one pattern: ritual. They purport to show how worship may be "enriched." They follow generally the teachings of experience gained through historical liturgical practices or they seek to relate the forms of worship to psychological needs. There is no disparagement of the worth of such studies, but there are defects and limitations which these pages attempt to point out. It is similarly true that much is being written on ecumenicity. The distinctiveness of the chapter herein on this subject lies in that which is almost invariably omitted. That is that ecumenicity is so restricted that it belies its name and loses much of its significance.

Finally there is the recognition that even the most thorough and capable studies and evaluations of the Christian church shy away from ultimate logical deductions perhaps because the authors purposely confine themselves to the immediacies believing that they alone are profitable considerations or because their sanguine souls create an aura of optimism about all that bears a holy name. In contrast the writer of these pages believes that it is necessary to look beyond the horizon to appraise values, attitudes and duties of the present.

Thus the aim in presentation in these chapters is to include with facts often related some that are missed, but are important, to gather into one, separated facts that their cumulative force may be felt and to discover the inferences that should be drawn from them.

Chapter I

BACKGROUNDS

Backgrounds are important. Sources are even more important. If we are to make any appraisal of American Protestantism we must have some idea not only of America —that perhaps we need not supply copiously—but also of the church before the Reformation. We must follow, too, the meandering stream sometimes subterranean and invisible that issued into the deep river of Protestantism in our country. The detailed accuracy of historical research may be left to scholars who have portrayed vividly the story of Christianity. There remain, however, certain brief summations and inferences that make for interpretation.

Any careful reader of the New Testament will perceive that the apostolic church was more of a gelatinous substance than a skeletal structure. Organization was inchoate. The church sprang from a kind of spontaneous necessity. The group of believers held something in common that virtually compelled them to meet together. A new religious direction derived from association with Jesus supplied the primary impulse. Their firm belief that Jesus had conquered death supplied the spark to set them in motion. They were Jews and originally had no thought of breaking away completely from temple and synagogue. Indeed they carried over something of the ideas of the temple and the usages of the synagogue into the Christian churches. But this was later. In the beginning they were not at all sure that mundane affairs would not come to a speedy end with some sort of a triumphant reappearance of Jesus. Meantime they met in simple fashion reading the Scriptures as they had been accustomed to do for the Old Testament then as now was considered a book of divine inspiration. They sang. They prayed. They talked. One custom established relatively early was unique. They partook of bread and wine in commemoration of the Last Supper. Apparently this observance was connected with a common meal. That itself would indicate informality. What leadership existed seemed to be supplied by the apostles—the chosen men who had been close to Jesus. All this is evident to any reader of the New Testament. Naturally in the earliest years the chief center was Jerusalem. As time went on the church grew. Some organization was demanded. The first trace of organization was not the result of any premeditation or imposed theory. It was practical in origin. It arose from circumstances of administering funds for the needy. That this might be systematized and supervised so that there would be fairness in distribution deacons were appointed to make the work their special care. Christianity not only grew numerically, it also spread geographically. The far flung churches consisted first principally of Jews. More and more Gentiles were received. The Apostle Paul was not the pioneer in establishing Gentile churches but his efforts extended the number of such churches and his interpretation of Christianity loosed the cords that bound Christianity to the Jewish faith and it expanded into a universal religion. Naturally organization was required. It is not surprising that there was not uniformity in development. Canon Streeter maintains that Episcopal, Presbyterian and Independent usages have equal claim to whatever authority attaches to primitiveness. Presbyters and bishops are mentioned in the later books of the New Testament. Obviously no distinctive priestly powers inhered in the offices, but there was the seed from which clericalism eventually sprang. Similarly the simple eucharist developed into formalism. The word eucharist came from the prayer of thanksgiving modeled after the giving of thanks by Jesus at the Last Supper. By the end of the first century there were formal prayers used in this connection. The Epistle of Ignatius (110-177 A.D.) holds that the eucharist is not to be celebrated without a bishop, but there seem to have been informal eucharistic prayers still. Iraenius (180 A.D.) says that Christ acknowledged the bread to be His body, the wine His blood. The eucharist had been severed from the common meal and had become a separate sacrificial ceremony. Cyril of Jerusalem notes an effect produced by consecration of the elements similar to the transformation of water into wine by our Lord at Cana.

It was in such a manner that not only was spiritual food transformed in the teaching of the church into a literal partaking of the body and blood of Christ, but liturgy grew and simple leaders became clothed with priestly power that separated them from the laity. Bishops were at first local. Gradually there came to exist the three orders of bishops, presbyters, and deacons. Probably the germ of what has subsequently become the doctrine of apostolic succession came into being through practical reasons. When an heretical sect like the Gnostics laid claim to doctrines going back to the Apostle Peter, the church could counter with apostolic sanction for the appointment of bishops. It should be observed that such officers made no pretension to powers claimed by later bishops and also that primacy lay not in a particular bishop—of Rome for example—for bishops were local and theoretically equal. But the bishops did eventually become priests, with distinctive authority, and the simple breaking of bread was changed into a sacrament. As the church organization was solidified its boasted catholicity was attained by the process of excluding all who deviated from the official norm. Emerging from the long period of persecution, the church in time became intolerant of dissent.

At the beginning of the fourth century Constantine was

3

enthroned emperor of Rome and granted toleration to the Christian church and then professing Christianity himself lifted it to a privileged position. The effects were obvious. The church gained tremendous prestige. Its growth and prosperity were assured. But inevitably the church became a worldly institution mixed inextricably with the politics of Rome and Christianity was soon the religion of the state.

Constantine, emperor, took upon himself authority to summon councils of the church. It was thus that the Nicene creed was adopted. The same council recognized the claims to primacy of the bishop of Rome in the west. The decisions of the council of Nicaea were promulgated as imperial law. Thus not only were state and church united but the state was seen as superior in power.

It was this century, too, that witnessed the growth of monasticism. Hermits who withdrew from the world and the worldliness of the church to live austere lives in isolation were succeeded by orders of monks. They were men who withdrew into monasteries where celibacy, obedience and poverty were accepted as the rule of their lives.

The Roman empire had been divided into an eastern dominion with its capital Byzantium, afterwards re-named Constantinople, and a western where Rome continued its domination, challenged by barbarians who eventually took over and became the rulers. In these changeful times the Church was the stabilizing force. It was natural that with the advance of episcopacy the prestige of the "Eternal City," Rome, should enhance the position of the Bishop of Rome. It was Leo, called the Great, bishop of Rome, 440-461, who envisaging an ecclesiastical monarchy, made the first claims for the supremacy of the Roman see and became the first real Pope.

The Emperor Justinian sent his armies from the East to conquer Italy. The State exercised control of the Church,

4

but also became the champion of orthodoxy. Heretics were put to death.

In the year 590 Gregory the Great came to the papal chair. His vigorous reforms and energetic politics put the church into first place in Italy and the West. His credulity in respect of miracles and his veneration of relics are signs of the way the church had taken. The period in general is notable for three things: The order the church was able to impose upon the barbarians, whose incursions were destined to change Europe drastically; the extension of Roman Christianity through missionary effort; and the schism that separated the eastern church from the west. Differences political, theological, and ecclesiastical had long existed between the two sections of the empire which were nominally one, as the church was nominally one. As usual, the causes of difference were mixed, but of interest to this study is the controversy over the use of images in worship. Leo, called the Isaurian, an emperor of the east, who had halted the Moslem advance, turned to reforms in the church. Mohammedanism, which had made such headway against idolatry, pointed a finger of scorn at the church for its use of images. Leo forbade (726) the use of images in worship. The practice, however, was deeply rooted and the pope Gregory II declined to obey. The controversy continued for years and found its climax in the separation of the churches of the east from the dominion of the pope at Rome. Thus was consummated the great schism in the church.

In order to understand the course of the church in these almost fantastic developments from the simplicity of Apostolic times, it should be noted that in exchange for papal favors in the recognition of his dynasty, Pepin the Frank granted the pope political and territorial authority in Ravenna. It was thus that the pope first acquired temporal dominion.

Pepin's son, known to history as Charlemagne, extended his empire to nearly all of western Europe, including the northern half of Italy. On Christmas, 800, the emperor knelt at the altar in prayer and the pope, Leo III, placed the imperial crown upon his head. Charlemagne did not know of the intention of the pope to crown him as emperor, but could scarcely do other than acquiesce. Factually, it was Charlemagne who was supreme, but the coronation offered an implication, that ecclesiastics were not loath to draw in time, that the spiritual head, in placing the crown upon Charlemagne's brow, acted as the one who, deriving power directly from God, held authority over temporal princes. Whatever might be the divine right of kings, it was dependent in its recognition upon the vicar of God. There was established, at any rate, a new empire that was to hold the luster of the Roman name and be definitely Christian in profession.

The Carolingian empire soon disintegrated. When Otto the Great was crowned by the pope the Holy Roman Empire expressed in its name an ideal or theory, but not an actuality. The empire did not coincide with Christendom. Indeed, feudalism created a social and economic change in Europe. In theory, the pope was the spiritual, the emperor the temporal head of Christendom.

The story of the church and what it came to mean is made clear by conditions and claims that evolved from this somewhat undefined relation between church and empire. There was admitted corruption in the monasteries and among the clergy, but even a pope inclined to reforms found his intentions impeded by the intermixture of spiritual and political authority. A bishop because of his office would appear to be subject to the control of the church, but if he had extensive holdings of land as he often had, the question of who held the spiritual office was a matter of concern to the temporal power. When the bishop was appointed by the

6

king, it certainly complicated matters. Hildebrand, who became Pope Gregory VII was a reformer. It was logical from the papal point of view to claim for the spiritual potentate supremacy over the political monarch. Was not the pope the representative of God as no emperor or king could be? Did he not possess the rights guaranteed to him as the successor of Peter, to whom were given the keys of the kingdom of God? When such assumptions were made, it was inevitable that they should come into conflict with imperial claims and ambitions. In the struggle, the advantage was with the pope. The zenith of papal power was attained when an emperor stood as a penitent, asking the forgiveness of the pope and accepting the claim of the pope to be the judge of kings.

We may inject here a few lines of comment germane to the almost incredible change wrought in the church since the days of the Apostles. The emergence of the stupendous papal claim of sovereignty is in amazing contrast to the attitude of the lowly Jesus, who said his kingdom was not of this world, meaning apparently that it was spiritual, not political. The difference needs but to be mentioned to display the contrast. There is an equal though not inexplicable contrast in the ideals of piety. Jesus and his great apostle, Paul, to take him as a typical example, lived simply among the people, interested in serving them. It was characteristic of Jesus that he went about doing good. As Christianity grew into worldly dominance with political ambitions, the most earnest believers withdrew from the world to lead ascetic lives of contemplation in monasteries and convents. It was later that such orders as the Dominicans and Franciscans sought to combine the two principles of asceticism and monastic seclusion with service to the people. But preaching friars did not displace the older orders of more strict seclusion. The Crusades offer a third contrast. Undoubtedly these astonishing religious expeditions were motivated by a variety of impulses and ambitions. The ostensible

7

motive and the really religious one was a desire to snatch the so-called holy places commemorative of the life and death of Christ from the grasp of Mohammedans, infidels from the Christian point of view. It is beyond conception that Jesus would ever have led or sanctioned the use of armies to accomplish such a purpose.

In following the record of the papacy, we note it ebbs and flows in its influence. So low did the institution fall that for years it was subservient to the kings of France and its seat was removed from Rome to Avignon. History also discloses to us the spectacle of two popes each claiming to be legitimate and hurling anathemas at the other. After this sorry chapter, history resumes the narrative of the popes in Rome, but it is mostly an unsavory mess about occupants of the papal throne who were devoid of both religion and morals.

On the better side, there should be related the theory of the church developed by thinkers of no mean ability, that the whole Christian community was united in and by faith; thus the chief end of man was to love and obey God and that human institutions and society should be patterned after these basic conceptions. In order to make all this practical, the church developed and ordained sacramental means to meet completely the exigencies of life. The medieval individual was brought to the Church and to God by baptism soon after birth. Adolescence was marked by confirmation, through which the Christian motive was brought before him and strengthened in him. His daily life was regulated through confession of his sins to a priest and the penance exacted because of the sins. In the church he regularly received the communion which meant to him that his Savior was brought to him literally in the bread and the wine. When he came to marry, he entered into the marital relation through the sacrament of the church that brought the home and family under divine jurisdiction. At the end of life he was prepared for his exit from the world by extreme unction administered by the priest. If holy orders and especially the monastic ideal proclaimed a higher life and divided Christian people into an upper and lower order spiritually, it was also true that for the ordinary man the secular was supposed to be governed by the spiritual. With what goodness and badness men actually lived during the middle ages is an entirely different matter. That corrupt living was not unknown to the clergy, entered the monasteries, and disclosed its most atrocious examples among the popes is something already indicated, but the political ambition, the infidelity and the utter moral degradation of the worse popes are almost incredible. That the same laxity percolated through to bishops, the ordinary clergy and the monks is what one would expect. So against the complete sacramental provision for secular life there must be set the fact that even in the most religious periods of the middle ages the people generally were ignorant, superstitious, crude, gross and of neither a spiritual nor moral calibre to command the admiration of subsequent generations.

Thus briefly we have reviewed the stupendous changes in the church and in its interpretation of Christianity from the days of the apostles through the middle ages. Then like a slow, scarcely noticeable leak followed by a bursting of a dam, a new world comes upon us in the Renaissance. The Renaissance forms the immediate background for the Protestant Reformation.

The Renaissance cannot be understood primarily as the result of a series of separate if related events. First of all it must be understood as a manifestation of what human nature is. We well know that Greece and Rome in ancient days produced a civilization that still casts its spell upon man and has its continuing effect upon our language and ideas. Whatever may have been the internal causes of the decadence of the Roman empire, the external forces were enough to insure its collapse. Mass after mass of crude, untutored but physically vigorous tribes of barbarians from western Europe rushed across its borders with an impact like successive waves of an angry sea. The structure of early civilization, already weakened, crumbled under barbarian attacks. The resulting process of race and ideological assimilation was necessarily a long one. The church became more dogmatically impervious to new ideas and suspicious of secular knowledge. Thus the naturally slow process was more retarded. There were events of great moment such as the fall of Constantinople with the consequent spread of ancient manuscripts in the west, that are closely related to the period that has been called the Renaissance, but the real explanation is more fundamental in human nature. The process of transforming hordes originally barbarous into civilized peoples was virtually completed. Repressed human nature reasserted itself. As the intellectual wealth of the ancients trickled in the ecclesiastical barriers crumbled. A flood of creative genius was released. Art and literature flourished, scholarship responded to new incentives and new opportunities; all heuristic impulses were stimulated. The thought and life of churchmen were affected.

To hold that the Protestant Reformation was just a part of the Renaissance is to misunderstand both. There were really three principal streams the confluence of which produced the great Protestant movement. The first was intellectual. In this sense Protestantism was largely, not entirely, a by-product of the Renaissance. New universities were founded. Scholars like Colet and Erasmus became interested in manuscripts of the Bible and in re-examination of religious doctrines. Martin Luther although he was not a scholar of the first rank, gave himself to the study of the apostle Paul, Augustine and others. In the congenial atmosphere of the time he pondered the dogmas of the church. The critical faculty held in restraint was freed to roam

10

about almost at will. Of course there were limits. Galileo expressing the new theories of science met the displeasure of the church. The new spirit of eager and critical inquiry raised fundamental questions about authority in religion. It induced a more zealous study of the Bible. Luther's conclusion that "the just shall live by faith" was the result of study and reflection. So was his question about authority and his appeal from the authority of the pope to that of a council, although that was influenced by practical exigencies. When, a little later, John Calvin wrote his "Institutes" it was evident that the Reformation was departing from the thought forms of the Roman church. Indeed before Calvin both Zwingli and Luther had denied the doctrine of transubstantiation. Luther in substituting consubstantiation for transubstantiation was less radical than Zwingli, who made the communion service one of commemoration only but it is an illustration of the intellectual element that entered and ran through the Protestant Reformation. It was thus in part a response to the new knowledge and the intellectual impetus furnished by the times.

The second stream that in conjunction with the others issued in the Reformation might be called the spiritual. During the later period of the middle ages as we have noted the church became corrupt in its life. Formalism united with ignorance and intolerance made a travesty of the Christianity induced by the New Testament in its story and its teaching. However, there were living flowers in what often seemed a mass of putrefaction. There is a continuous if not always connected record of saintliness. There were great souls within the church of Rome. There were great souls who were forced out of it or fled from it. In general, it may be said that these men had one thing in common: They were followers of the inner light. Some, not all, could be ranked as mystics, but all cherished a religion of experience apart from though by no means always in contradis-

11

tinction to the formalities of the church. Examples may be selected almost at random. Within the church and not questioning its doctrines the two most notable were Bernard of Clairvaux and Francis of Assisi. These two were different in many ways, but had much in common. Bernard was given the designation of Clairvaux because that was the monastery with which he was long connected as abbot. He was born in 1091. His adult life was spent as a zealous and reforming monk. Turning from the lax and rich monasteries that then flourished, he went to Citeaux which had the reputation of strict observance of the rules of monastic life. From there he went to Clairvaux to establish a monastery, also of the strictest order. In many ways Bernard was at one with the time in which he lived. As a monk he subjected himself to austerities that were severe. As a thinker he was a staunch defender of the faith. No taint of "heresy" ever touched him. Rather he was the soul of orthodoxy. The contemplative life of the monastery did not expel the desire to serve. He was a preacher of power. He intervened on one occasion to save Jews from massacre by an infuriated mob under a fanatical leader. That which is most attractive in the story of Bernard was the spiritual quality of his life. He was simple-hearted. He personified the rare combination of boldness against wrong with gentleness. The real greatness of Bernard was in the simple and sincere beauty of his religious life. To him religion bore fruit in deeds, but the roots were deep in the heart. While to others religion was a cloak lightly worn and if inconvenient gayly discarded, to him it was life and light. He cherished and developed this life of the spirit.

Francis, born in 1182, different though he was from Bernard, was one with him in spiritual devotion. This gay young man was transformed by a profound spiritual experience, turned from his wealth and luxurious living to follow a life of poverty, spiritual devotion and service. He gathered some of like mind about him. From this association there came the order of preaching friars known as Franciscans. The ideas of Francis worked out in the order he founded, were that the life of contemplation should be united with that of active ministry to the people. The monastery walls did not separate those within from those without as in the older orders. The humility and sincerity of Francis shone on a cold dark world like stars in a frosty night. His delightful relation with the birds, the sun, the moon, showed his belief that this is "my Father's world." The intensity of his devotion to Christ and the cross was saved from fanaticism by just such simple joy and friendliness toward the created world. All in all, Francis of Assisi was an example of piety at its best. Forgetful of self, sympathetic with human need, cultivating a spirit of worship, he is unsurpassed in the galaxy of spiritual heroes. Not only is he a witness to the enduring vitality of Christian truth, but a link in the golden chain that connected the Christ of the gospels with a really Christian community of later generations.

Peter Waldo belongs to the twelfth century. His life was a protest primarily against the loose living of the clergy. It was an attempt to recapture the simplicity and devoutness of the early Christians. The call he sounded to this kind of life met a response from many of like mind. Originally from Lyon, France, they were involved with the Albigenses, a sect accused of heresy and exterminated in one of the most determined expeditions of persecution ever undertaken through the stimulation of the church. Some of the followers of Waldo escaped and found refuge in the mountains of northern Italy, whence it was impossible to dislodge them. Their descendants are in Italy to this day and form now a body of indigenous Protestants. They turned to the repudiation of transubstantiation, the adoration of the Virgin and the Saints and to other positions subsequently assumed by Protestantism. A few in France somehow outlived the persecution there and eventually merged with the Calvinists of that country. Although the Waldenses, as they came to be called, were in much of their thinking classified as heretics, they have drawn attention principally because of the sincerity, earnestness and purity of their lives and the zeal of their preaching.

John Tauler of the fourteenth century was a Dominican who lived in Strassburg. He was an eloquent preacher who at times put his conscience above the edicts of the church, as when although the city was under a papal interdict, he continued to minister to the sick and the dying. Tauler's emphasis was upon inward religion. He repeatedly called upon his hearers to turn from images and pictures and created things to God himself. The story of John Tauler is particularly interesting for two reasons. The first is that of his relation to a group of people living mostly in Switzerland who have been known as Friends of God. Tauler was greatly influenced by these men and women who were believers in the religion of the Spirit and put their beliefs into practice. They are an illustration of groups rather vaguely known who made religion a spiritual reality— something to be lived. The second reason is that Martin Luther definitely acknowledged the influence of Tauler upon him.

The same kind of phenomenon is to be recognized in England. John Wyclif was born in Yorkshire in the early part of the fourteenth century. He was a scholar and a theologian. Denouncing the conduct of the monks, questioning and denying the doctrines of the church, he would assuredly have met an untimely fate had he not received powerful political protection. His greatest achievement was the translation of the Bible into English. He well deserved the name that later generations bestowed upon him, "The Morning Star of the Reformation." His followers were known as Lollards. They went through England preaching. The

14

Lollards were finally repressed but never entirely extinguished until they merged with the men and women of the Protestant Reformation. It is interesting and important to note that the influence of Wyclif crossed into the continent and was conspicuous in the life and work of John Hus and his followers in Bohemia. It should be added that many of these groups were intent on returning to the simplicity of the primitive church.

It is evident that during even the darkest centuries when the Roman church was at its lowest the light of true religion still shone and indeed the torch was passed on from generation to generation. These tiny lights ignited a conflagration when circumstances combined to give occasion and opportunity.

There was a third cause of the Protestant Reformation. It was the realization of the need of reform of a church that exhibited spiritual and moral decadence. This penned-up indignation awaited some concrete event that would be sufficiently flagrant and conspicuous to furnish occasion for an outburst of reforming zeal. This was furnished by the appearance in Germany of a monk, named Tetzel, who was little better than a peddler of indulgences. It was the time of the building of Saint Peter's cathedral in Rome. Money was required for the enormous expense of its erection. One of the methods chosen for raising money was the sale of indulgences. This promised to have a popular appeal as the nature of an indulgence was such as to stir emotions often sheathed in superstition. The doctrine of indulgences was built upon a belief that Christ and later holy men had accumulated a large surplus supply of merits that were available to others at the discretionary disposal of the church. The indulgence was a remission of penalties for sins other than mortal and its efficacy extended into purgatory. In theory the indulgence presupposed repentance, but a good salesman like Tetzel could not be expected to

15

stress the hard requirements, but make his appeal to the emotions of prospective customers. It was a popular belief that the purchase of an indulgence would release the soul of a departed loved one from purgatory. Some appear to have thought that "if they bought letters of indulgence they are sure of their final salvation," so Luther wrote. Apparently Tetzel was a salesman, not a teacher. Martin Luther was indignant at the sight of Tetzel playing upon the superstitions and emotions of the common people in what were considered the sacred things. Luther was himself a monk in whose mind there had been questions about doctrines and their reason and in his heart was uneasiness over the corrupt practices of the church, although until pushed by one crisis after another he had been an obedient son of the church. As a protest against the performances of Tetzel, Luther posted ninety-five theses on the door of the church at Wittenberg on the subject of indulgences. That meant that he was prepared to defend his statements by argument. He did not lack opponents! He was forced through debate from one position to another. Affirming that a general council was of greater authority than the pope, he admitted that councils had erred. In attacking the pope and admitting that the councils were not inerrant Luther was soon in a position of rebellion. He went so far as to assail the Roman church and even advocate a national German church. This was in accord with the spirit of nascent nationalism. He lessened the distinction between priest and layman, alleging that it was of function not of estate, and that the mind of Christ is the possession of all Christians who therefore may understand the Word of God. He repudiated the sacrifice of the mass, the doctrine of transubstantiation and argued for the priesthood of all believers and for justification by faith. Naturally such a course could not be followed with impunity. Condemnatory papal bulls were burned just as Luther's books were burned by the other side. Before the Imperial Diet of

Worms Martin Luther faced his accusers and the emperor himself. He refused to recant. Instead he made his world-shaking affirmation: "Here I take my stand. I can do no other." As a result he was declared an outlaw of the empire and was excommunicated by the church. However, he had powerful protection and escaped. Churches repudiating the authority of Rome were formed. It was after this that he translated the New Testament into German. This was significant in that it was a move in advancing the scriptures to the place they assumed in the reformed churches.

It was an anomaly that the German princes should have the determination of the form of religion that should prevail in their respective states. However, the gain of this concession advanced the cause of the Reformation. Later when the emperor Charles V was in a stronger position this was withdrawn. In consequence the princes who adhered to Lutherism protested. From this protest the name Protestant arose and was applied to the new churches. It is a mistake, due perhaps to propaganda, to infer that Protestantism was just a negative achievement. On the contrary, it was based on a great declaration of Luther in quoting from the New Testament: "The just shall live by faith." This became the watchword of the Reformation. It was an affirmation. So was the belief in the competency of the lay Christian to interpret the scriptures for himself. So was the assertion of the authoritativeness of the Bible. So was the insistence on the priesthood of all believers. The word "Protestant" is thus a misnomer with its negative connotation as applied to the churches that were born of the Reform movement.

It was inevitable both logically and historically that numerous denominations should spring up as the result of the Reformation. If the individual conscience was accepted as the determinant then every group was entitled to its peculiar ideas. Fear, caution, conservatism, prevented the new churches from accepting the full logic of their position:

the absolute liberty of conscience. The Ana-Baptists were the exception and were persecuted for their logic. The reformers generally had a wholesome fear of religious anarchy. Historical situations were often decisive in the formation of churches. This was notable first in England where Henry VIII pushed his matrimonial plans until they collided with the policies if not the principles of the pope. He therefore compelled the Church of England to secede from papal jurisdiction and assumed its headship himself. Protestant influences were at work in England and it must not be inferred that the English church was merely the creation of her monarch, but its particular form was the result of the English historical situation. Nearby Scotland fell under the ecclesiastical domination of John Knox, who in turn had fallen under the spell of John Calvin and the Presbyterian form of government. Naturally most German churches were molded by the teachings and organization of Martin Luther. Diversity is the price we pay for liberty.

As time went on sects multiplied wherever there was freedom. Even where freedom was limited they sprang up. Logically, as we have seen, freedom was inherent in Protestantism from its inception. But logic has a hard time against prejudice. It is not easy for human beings to see that flourish in which they disbelieve and even hold to be detrimental to the people. With the cocky assurance that most men have that they are right and that all who differ with them are obviously wrong, it is difficult to accord dissidents a right to their own beliefs and practices. Therefore, religious liberty although it began a lusty growth after the Reformation was soon struggling with restraining devices applied to prevent its advancing. In England, for example, from which most of the Protestant shoots that grew in America were transplanted, it was long before complete freedom of religion was admitted.

With all the diversities, compromises, limitations, there

were some possessions common to the churches of the new order generally. There was a sincere desire to recapture reality. This does not mean that Protestantism automatically weeded out time-servers, politicians, professional reformers. King Henry IV of France did not hold soul-gripping convictions as a Protestant or he would not have concluded that a kingdom was worth a mass. It does mean a desire to scrape off accretions that hid reality as lichen hides the rocks it covers, to reach the truth beneath. There was the desire to recover Christianity in its purity and the church as it was before politics, historical changes, ignorance, superstition, clericalism, corruption, had so fastened themselves upon it as to hide and disfigure it. The very multiplicity of sects bore witness to the intentness of those who pursued the project of reclamation.

The churches born of the reform movement displayed a common awareness of the present. They perceived that the decadent church did not and could not effectively minister to human need. And of human need they were keenly aware. As was the church, so largely were the people. They, too, were ignorant, superstitious, immoral—not all, it should be added. The common people as always had their problems of living. Birth, death, family, livelihood, inevitably imposed the need of spiritual guidance and help. Religion must be simplified, brought within their grasp, applied to the practical demands of their lives. To that end the new churches emphasized preaching. The translation of the Bible into the vernacular was for the instruction of the common people, not for the edification of scholars. Most notable were Luther's translation into German and Tyndale's translation into English. Tyndale's expressed wish that every ploughboy should know his Bible came near to fulfillment. The German Bible largely molded the modern German tongue, the English Bible wove itself into the common speech of the people. In the translated Bibles the

19

artisan, the farmer as well as the socially and intellectually elite could have recourse to the Word of God, from which they might gain direct instruction and comfort. The Bible was open on the pulpit and open in the home. The prophet in the pulpit tended to supersede the priest at the altar.

In general, the churches of the Reformation also were gifted with a look toward the future. Roman Catholicism has always tried primarily to maintain the idea of an organization that was infallible and to that extent perfect. The Protestant churches although each one was disposed to set claims to superiority as the true reproduction of the allegedly pure primitive church, were really pressing toward a goal. The very multiplication of sects is evidence of unsatisfactory longing, a striving for perfection. The Council of Trent purged the Catholic church of many abuses, but carefully reset it on the old foundations. The pietistic movement on the continent and the various succeeding forms of Puritanism in England were efforts toward new attainments in Protestantism. The Catholic church shared missionary advance with Protestantism, but it is not too much to make the perennial distinction that Catholicism wished as always to extend itself as an institution in order that people might be saved, while Protestants tried to save people and the building up of its own churches thereby was quite subordinate—a characteristic that unhappily is not universally in evidence in American church life.

Most of the leading sects developed in America had their origin in England. From an early period dissent is found in that country. In the Church of England itself there was division. The Protestant teachings and influences penetrated the church that Henry VIII had made emphatically nationalistic. The Puritans were bent on reformation of life and liturgy. They moved farther away from Rome and were all for removing Roman taints from the Church. They were inclined to sobriety and severity in their outlook upon life, and were advocates of that practice in personal conduct. The Puritans, as they have been called who settled at Massachusetts Bay, became independents upon American soil.

More extreme Puritanism was the rule in the dissenting churches that sprang up in England. But more than the independent churches Presbyterianism for a short time strove for control of the English state. When James I came down from Scotland to assume the English crown, it naturally widened the doorway through which Presbyterianism, regnant in the northern country, could enter England. At the time of the Puritan Revolution Presbyterianism clutched at the superior power in England. The Independents, however, were more important for American history. Under the leadership of Browne there was an assertion by congregations of Christians of a radical turn who held that the church should be free from coercion and control by the State and instead of episcopal government as in the Church of England or government by presbyteries, as in the Presbyterian communion, each local congregation should be self-governing. These churches became known in time as Congregational because the control was in the congregation. Closely related to these independent churches were the Baptists. They were the spiritual descendants of the Ana-Baptists of the Reformation, but there seems to be no direct historical connection. The Ana-Baptists were the radicals of Protestantism. They refused to compromise and, undeterred by practical considerations, followed the road of logic all the way. If Protestantism substituted private judgment for ecclesiastical authority the only possible deduction was that every individual should be allowed to exercise freedom of conscience. So it was that Hübmaier, their most notable leader, wrote a tract insisting that heretics should be convinced by reason and not persecuted. Their habit of baptizing, not always by immersion, upon confession of faith upon the part of the one seeking baptism stemmed naturally from their belief in the spiritual sovereignty of the individual. Some of the Ana-Baptists in later years were accused of fanaticism and extreme political and social ideas. They were exterminated or died out except for a few who emigrated to Pennsylvania and then as Mennonites perpetuated the faith of their fathers. The English Baptists separated themselves from the other Independents in adopting the fundamental ideas and practices of the Ana-Baptists.

Two other denominations were of later origin: the Quakers and the Methodists. The followers of John Fox formed the Society of Friends, whose principal distinctive tenet was a firm belief in "the inner light," that is the Spirit of God in the life of the believer, as the ultimate authority—a belief incidentally in which they were anticipated by some of the Ana-Baptists. The Methodists were first the fire-bringers to the church of England at the time dormant in frigid intellectualism. John Wesley influenced by the Moravians, a notable group of genuinely pious continentals, took his fervor, generated by a real spiritual experience, to the Church of England where his unwonted zeal and unconventional methods were not welcomed. Eventually the followers of Wesley were compelled to begin an independent communion.

Such were the various sects that were transplanted in America. In Virginia it was the Church of England. In Massachusetts it was the Puritans who became independent and eventually formed the Congregational Church. Roger Williams, driven from Massachusetts because of his views, established the first Baptist church in the new world in Rhode Island. The Quakers found a home in Pennsylvania. Reformed churches from the continent of Europe followed the Dutch who settled in New York and New Jersey. Wesley himself made a trip to America and in time Methodists were to be counted among American churches, whose heroic pioneer on the western continent was Francis Asbury. Presbyterianism filtered in for the Scotch-Irish were numerous in some sections.

Such migrations of churches were to be expected in a new world consisting of settlements made by many divergent groups. The really significant observation to be made is that there was the congenial climate for Protestantism that developed after the Colonies became an independent nation. In the colonial days and extending far into the history of the United States, America was predominantly Protestant. The only colony that in any sense could be considered Catholic was Maryland, where Lord Baltimore, himself a Catholic, opened a haven for Catholics who still had no freedom in England. In order to gain permission for his enterprise of inviting Catholics to the colony, Lord Baltimore was compelled to grant freedom to Protestants also. So America had no such tussle with Roman Catholic intolerance as had the countries of Europe where the Catholic church was in control before the agonizing struggle of the Reformation successfully challenged the absoluteness of that church. However, religious freedom was not indigenous to colonial soil. State supported churches in Massachusetts for example survived the American Revolution and the adoption of the United States constitution with its Bill of Rights that was attached to the original document soon after that became the fundamental law of the land.

The guarantee of religious liberty and the prohibition of an established church reflected not only Protestant sentiment, but created a condition in which Protestantism with its strength and weaknesses might thrive. The constitutional provision against any religious establishment gave rise to the American doctrine of the separation of state and church. This doctrine accepted by virtually all Protestants, became the bulwark of free religion. There would be no fostering of any church by the government and there would be no governmental interference with any church. It was precisely

23

the climate needed for the expansion of Protestant churches. The migration westward that characterized the 19th century culminated in the linking of the Atlantic coast with the Pacific by means of the railways. That achievement made the country one in a new and permanent sense. But the process of western expansion had a strong influence upon religion and the churches. The new west, slowly and steadily extended, ever invited the adventurous who were lured by the uninhabited spaces into the belief that it was better farther on. It is evident that these bold spirits whose security rested upon their vigilance, adaptability, and self-reliance formed the vanguard of an army of democracy. Independence and liberty were the qualities that were a natural part of life on the frontier. It was the west that made the new nation really democratic. Protestantism in America not only found its opportunity in such an atmosphere, but its growth was affected by it. The American churches were imbued with the spirit of democracy and liberty. Even churches whose government was not theoretically democratic in practice emulated the democratic way. Denominations that abroad might be State Churches who rather grudgingly allowed dissenters to exist, in America became as stout defenders of liberty of conscience as the most radical independent. Since in America no church could look to the public treasury for support, none was treated as an inferior. All this inevitably had a deplorable side. The United States became notorious for religious progeny whose raucous and often disputatious voices created an ecclesiastical bedlam. Sects, sects, sects everywhere!

The picture of Protestantism in America would not be complete without the mention of other groups that affect its coloring. First there are the Roman Catholics. They were relatively few until about the middle of the last century. Then there came the migration from Ireland, a staunchly

Catholic country, except for its strongly Protestant north. The Irish Catholics pushed ahead. In an extraordinarily short time these new citizens gained political control of many of the cities and reached out more and more to influence national politics and national life. The Catholic church began to pick up in America. Later there were surges of immigrants from southern Europe where the Catholic church was dominant. The Catholic church increased in number and prestige. It may be argued that the hierarchy of that church remained unchanged in ideology and convictions, but it is to be admitted that many of the lay people imbibed principles of American Protestantism and accept liberty of conscience as natural to America. Unfortunately, in the Catholic church lay opinion usually is easily stifled when the decisive moment arrives and the hierarchy exerts its pressure. Admittedly, the rise of Catholicism in America has pried Protestantism from its niche of security.

American Indians are not now a large enough section of the nation to be important and in the formative days of Protestantism they were affected by Christian teaching but did not affect it very much. Similarly the negroes, formerly a subordinate group, inherited the religion of their masters. They are numerous enough today and have made sufficient progress to make a possible contribution to the white churches, as indeed they have done in a minor way, through their spirituals. The present and proper tendency is to consider them less and less as a separate group.

The very large number of Jews in our country makes it necessary to speak of them in any adequate consideration of the conditions in which the Protestant churches have their life. Jews have come from many lands, driven by persecution or poverty and allured by prospects of freedom and prosperity. They are today so numerous and influential, especially in certain of our eastern cities, that politicians are forever on the watch lest they offend their Jewish constituents and so lose the Jewish vote, and hence, it may be, the election.

It is unfortunate that special interests form blocs that exist to influence legislation for their sole advantage. Everyone knows there are blocs representing industry, blocs representing organized labor, blocs representing the farmers. It is more lamentable that there should be religious blocs. All Protestants are not above fanaticism and organization to influence legislation, but the nature of Protestantism is such that it is impossible to hold more than a small minority in line politically even when the cause for which they are asked to unite is quite unselfish. The situation is different in respect of Catholics and Jews. In America there are Catholics who insist upon independence and who refuse to be dominated by clerical influence, but such is the strength of the Catholic church exercised through the unique powers ascribed to its priesthood, that on matters in which the hierarchy is interested pressure can be exercised upon the Catholic laity that few dare to defy. So upon certain issues there is a Catholic bloc. The majority of Jews are so fascinated with the movement known as Zionism that the foreign policy of the American government has descended to the political arena, where champions of both the parties have vied with each other in attempting to capture the so-called Jewish vote. That vote apparently was determined not at all by the interest or international ethical responsibilities of this country, but by what Jews had made their own peculiar interest.

Thus the American principle that would divorce favoritism of any church from governmental prerogatives is not assurance either of the acquiescence of all religious bodies in the doctrine or of the superiority of politicians to temptation to truckle to religious special interests so as to

26

gain votes. It remains, however, as the open gate into that temple of liberty that Protestantism has built.

To complete the survey of the environment of the Protestant churches in America, there must be the recognition of the fact that there is a vast multitude of the irreligious. Some belong in this category because modern science has thrust question-marks into their thinking and they regard religion as outmoded. Some are so because they have made money their God. Some have succumbed to the secular spirit of the times and have become indifferent to all religion.

The America of today is a country of the Protestant traditions, of religious freedom where amazing material progress has seduced men from the service of religion. At the same time, this economic advance and social confusions and inequities present a challenge and an opportunity to the church. It is the purpose of the following pages to tell how the Protestant churches are behaving in this land of religious liberty and irreligious temptation. Protestantism has forged the weapons for a successful assault upon entrenched wrong. How is it using the weapons? Or is it not using them?

Chapter II

THE CHURCH GLORIOUS

It is the temptation and tendency of our somewhat flamboyant America to illustrate progress under such a figure as that of a procession with waving banners, headed by a band playing a Sousa march. So it is held, religion marches on. War with its consequent as well as attendant evils has, to be sure, somewhat jolted our wonted complacency. The perception that "evolution"—which once assumed the pretentious royalty of capital letters—must be printed in lower case type has caused the more thoughtful to revise their conclusions. We know we cannot longer rely upon certain if sometimes fluctuating progress. The Darwinian conception of the ascent of man from the inorganic was ceremoniously conducted into the realms of mental and spiritual life and hailed as the vicar of God on earth. It was illogical from the beginning to transfer a physical law to spiritual life. This is now ruefully conceded especially as we have had forced upon our attention the almost incredible depravity exhibited in "purges," concentration camps and crematory chambers to which the living have been consigned. Sadism is a comparatively new and extremely uncomfortable word. Indeed there has been such extreme reaction from the easy optimism of the recent generation that Barth, the European theologian, has enlisted cohorts of followers who proclaim anew human depravity and the consequent separation between God and man. So the situation in America is one in which the cheerleaders may merely pause for breath, but the more thoughtful have no heart for the expression of sanguine enthusiasm.

To appraise not only the state of religion and the church today, but even its assets requires sober, objective and discriminating consideration. We are a statistically-minded people. We allow conclusions drawn from questionnaires and polls to masquerade in the garb of pure science and defer to them with astonishing obsequiousness. Even universities will solemnly grant degrees to those who write theses based upon questionnaires. We are sometimes tempted to think that we are to have both government and education by questionnaire methods. There is admittedly a certain value in information obtained in this way. But it is limited and inexact, sometimes it may be misleading and false. The first gauge of religious progress that forces itself upon our attention is that of statistics involving a questionnaire method. Each year solemnly, often triumphantly, we have presented to us statistics of the gains or losses of Protestantism in the country. They may be taken for what they are worth. The number of members on the roll of a church is not a real index of the number of members the church actually possesses. There is variance in practice. A few churches are very strict in keeping their rolls and lop off names with severity if not with charity—boasting that their rolls are up-to-date. The wisdom or perhaps the superficiality of this procedure is more than offset by the larger number of churches that almost never drop a name, for size is their criterion of success, and size even unreal is a means of maintaining standing in the ecclesiastical world. Most churches are between these extremes. They periodically make some revision of their rolls, erasing names of those irretrievably lost to the church, but in charity and hope retaining the names of those who even years hence may possibly be reclaimed. The philosophy as well as the practice of the churches are an introduction to the study of statistics. It is obvious that the statistics are unreliable for even an external estimate. It is equally true that requirements of admission to churches vary and that no small number who may not have their names on the rolls of churches are none the less real Christians and many whose names are on the rolls should in all conscience be counted out of the church, for their church-going is perfunctory and their church-membership has not the least relation to their way of life. Similarly, people join churches for various reasons, some of them scarcely worthy of approbation. Not a few who are accepted into churches have a very faint idea of what Christianity is. There are churches with standards of admission that are almost purely theological; others have no standards at all. They will gather in all whose consent may be obtained.

Notwithstanding these grim facts, it is probably true that statistics of accessions and of church membership may reveal a trend. If there are very few accessions it is rather good evidence that the interest in religion is not wide, especially when it is known that the churches generally have not imposed more strict conditions for membership. If, on the other hand, accessions are numerous and church membership is increasing, and there is no apparent growing laxity upon the part of the churches, the increase will probably indicate some new interest in religion. For some years statistics have shown a steady increase in church membership. More than half the people of the United States are church members. Of these 35% are Protestants. This is in contrast with the 22% reported for 1890. It is hard to reconcile this with the admitted fact that in 1890 church-going was more a sign of respectability and that people went to church rather generally. At the earlier date churches that now make no attempt to hold an evening service could boast good congregations twice a day. To be sure church-going and church-membership are not the same. There is nothing prodigious about the rate of increase from year to year, but it is heartening so far as it has any meaning. Indubitably there is reason for encouragement when we compare the period following the second World War with that after the first. In the earlier period iconoclastical sophistication combined with sceptical indifference among the youth of the land. During this period in a leading New England college, from which in days gone by many ministers had been graduated, there was just one student for the ministry in the entire college of six hundred or eight hundred young men. Whatever may be the explanation the effects of the more recent war accentuated by the Korean action have been different. Apparently there has been a feeling that war has swept away so much of what had been considered the secure and accumulated possessions of civilization that men have been startled from complacency and have made an apprehensive inquiry about what if anything was left. Was there anything to be salvaged from the wreck of civilization? Was the new barque which necessity has caused us to build to be launched with the name "Hope" or "Despair" painted upon its hull? In these circumstances there has been a new sobriety in evidence as youth and maturity seek the meaning of life. Reports from colleges indicate that many young people are turning to religion. The presence of such books as "Peace of Mind" upon the list of "best sellers" and their maintenance of a place there month after month is amazing for such are not what are ordinarily classed as popular books. There is only one possible explanation: That thousands of people are so earnest in their search for peace that they eagerly turn to anything that offers them deliverance from their fears and anxieties. "Peace of Mind" is a presentation of religion in a broad sense in harmonious relations with modern psychology or more specifically, psychiatry. There is some reality back of these figures of growth.

To return from interpretation to statistics themselves, it should be noted that approximately 35% of our population are Protestants. The inference from a thoughtful consideration of tables of growth with all the wariness and caution that figures so gathered impose is creditable to the faithfulness and enterprise of the churches. Religion is not dead in America. The churches are achieving something.

We cannot, however, write figures on the blackboard, triumphantly point to them, and let it go at that. What is back of the figures? What possessions and services of the church are to be listed in an inventory of her spiritual riches? It would seem indisputable that evangelism should be first. If there were no gospel to proclaim there would be neither reason nor excuse for the existence of a church. Always there has been the declaration of a way of life, through Jesus Christ. It was from the preaching of this conviction at Pentecost that the church came to birth. Its name and history have been possible only because of the confidence that there was a Christian gospel. The teaching has often been warped. It has been wrapped in an externalism that sometimes completely hid it. It has been tainted by spiritual corruption. But somehow it has never been entirely lost or destroyed. What the Apostle Paul termed the "foolishness of the preaching" has ever been the chief benefit of the church to man. The church has a message.

Evangelism is a word of simple historical content. It holds the story of Jesus, his death upon the cross and the new life that he brought from death. The theological interpretation has not been so simple. It is, though, a phenomenon to be observed by any unbiassed reporter that similar transformation of life and development of character have been produced by divergent interpretations. A crude evangelism has often made converts who were not spiritually deficient and an evangelism that discards and despises the name and seems woven of catechetical responses and liturgical ornateness has developed men and women of real spiritual stature. There must be charity and breadth of judgment in appraising such values. We must not confuse the essential gospel with its varying means of declaration. Evangelism in the form of "revivals" connoted much repugnant not only to cultivated taste but to simple reason and decorum. Any social historian will recite the positive harm they have done. Anyone dealing with human minds will register vehement objections to certain revivalistic methods. In the period of the settlement of the West, circuit riding preachers who were usually emotional in their appeals along with camp-meetings were the chief means of taking religion to the pioneers. The camp-meetings were highly exciting and even produced nervous disorders. The epidemic of barking like a dog by those whose nerves gave way to the strain was probably the most extraordinary, but not at all the only manifestation of the harmful effects of camp-meetings western style. Yet it cannot be denied that this crude ministry of the gospel was a benefit to the rough and ready makers of the West. Evangelism in the United States has been a strange mixture. It should be remembered that Jonathan Edwards, whose sermons sometimes seemed to be diatribes but swayed the feelings of the congregation and have astonished subsequent readers with their fearfulness, was one of America's great thinkers. Dwight L. Moody moved his listeners with an exposition of the saving love of God, but only the hypercritical—of whom there are some—would refuse to acknowledge the power for good in Moody's preaching. After all the only fair criticism is not of the emotion, but of emotion divorced from volition and at war with intelligence. It should be remembered that Moody won the support of Henry Drummond the scientist whose theology could not coincide with the doctrines held by Mr. Moody. The complexity of evangelism in this country is further illustrated by the reminder that Moody, the preacher lacking in scholastic training and the exponent of an uncritical theology, was the founder of two great schools where boys and girls might receive the education he lacked, but under Christian influence.

33

The most striking example of the kind of evangelism deplored by the enlightened was that of the late Billy Sunday as he was universally called. His antics, his crudeness, his speech that often bordered on the sacrilegious, the overt commercialism of it all disgusted many. Indeed, it is no recommendation of an evangelist when the question of whether he did more good or harm is seriously discussed. But it is unquestionable that the preaching of Billy Sunday made converts the quality and permanence of whose religion have been thoroughly proved.

The point of this discussion is that whatever the vagaries of the preachers—and they were many—and however disreputable were some of their methods—and they were disreputable—that there was a core of truth in their messages. There is something common to the preaching from the pulpit, in the tent or "tabernacle," in the open air. This has been the presentation of Jesus Christ as the superlative earthly being and of divine powers somehow emanating from his cross. Veiled by theological obscurantism, wrapped in doctrines insulting to intelligence, distorted by grotesque interpretations, the Christian Church has still faithfully proclaimed the gospel. It is all very human—the disagreements, the polished discourse and the illiterate speech, the cold respectability and the fiery utterance, the address to reason touched or untouched by the exploitation of emotionalism. There have been lights and deep shadows, hilltops and abysses, turbid pools and clear streams. That is to be expected in this world. When we accept this fact we can recognize the reality of the gospel declared by the church. Refusing to be confounded by human errancy we glorify the church for its message of hope to those who dwell in despair. Jewels of truth are in earthen vessels, but they are jewels and they are there.

It is difficult and unnecessary to separate evangelism from missions. The urge that has sent out apostles in every age has been that of the gospel. Carey the shoemaker who became a linguist felt called to carry the news of Jesus Christ to "the heathen." Judson was moved to preach the way of salvation to peoples who had never heard of our Lord. Today missions have become a social and educational leaven in many lands. But they have not thereby lost their religion. Here before communism gained control was a school for boys and girls in a great city of China. Nearby there was a home and school for blind girls. A little farther off there was a hospital modern in its appointments with a Chinese Christian physician in charge caring for the ill and in its clinic rendering free service to multitudes of the poor. All this is missions. But the center of these diverse activities was the nearby Christian Church where the Chinese minister preached to a thousand of his fellow-countrymen even on the hottest day of summer. Back of school house, hospital and church is the Christian zeal of America. Statistics of converts are often impressive, but the influence of Christianity in the East goes far beyond statistics. China is still the most conspicuous example where Chiang Kai Shek, now in exile, who for long was the principal man in the country, and his talented wife, educated in America, are avowed Christians. In Japan Kagawa, trained in our country, is a Christian preacher and social worker whose influence extends throughout his native land and returns to the United States. The heart of his magnificent achievement is the preaching of the gospel.

As the foregoing paragraphs have indicated, the value of missions is not to be estimated solely by its evangelistic success. The roll of Christian universities, colleges and schools even down to kindergartens in non-Christian lands is a long one. Most of the graduates are inoculated with Christian ideas. As the principal of a boy's school in Palestine pointed out to the writer young men from leading Arab families were students there. They might not become Christian, but the Christian ethics imbibed in the mission school would remain with most of them all their lives. To-morrow many of these youths would have positions in the State and determine its policies. Everyone who has visited the East, or has read of it, must be aware of the appalling amount of disease that exists. The church has sent Christian physicians and has trained native doctors. The stories of Doctor Seagrave in Burma, of Doctor Schweitzer in Africa are intensely interesting. They reveal, too, what the church means to the world. Doctor Seagrave is an American. Doctor Schweitzer is a European. That reminds us that while it is Protestantism in America that is under consideration parenthetically it may be remarked that it cannot be understood in isolation from Protestantism in other parts of the world. When John the Baptist sent disciples to inquire of Jesus if he were indeed the Christ, Jesus did not give a categorical answer. Instead he told John's friends to tell their leader what they had witnessed—the blind saw, the cripples walked, the sick were healed. Today this is Christianity. And it is magnificent.

The Christian missionary has gone further and further. He has gone into the villages of poverty and filth, has taught the people how to live decently and with an increase of happiness. Uncontaminated milk to save the lives of babies, improved methods of agriculture that would bring a plentiful supply of food to the community, have not been beneath the thought and effort of the missionary. Cannibals have been transformed into devout Christians. Ancient cultures have been vitalized by Christian contacts, the outcasts, untouchables, have been received as brothers and have felt the pressure of a friendly hand. India has recently passed laws that may abolish caste as it now exists. But what did India care for its pariahs until the missionary began preaching and practicing the religion of love? Where did India's leaders receive the impulse toward reform but in the colleges and universities of Christian England and America? Gandhi with his life of sacrificial service and his movements of peace and of liberation from ancient wrongs was educated in England and acknowledged his debt to Christian teaching.

The excesses of evangelists have discredited the old assumption that the health and growth of the church were dependent upon these periodic attempts to lure by organized emotionalism the recalcitrant and the indifferent into the fold. Churches have become more staid, formal, ritualistic. The study of social psychology has increased restraint. The churches generally no longer let themselves go in a fervent quest for souls. In the broad sense the gospel is still preached. Jesus Christ is presented as the hope of the world. Visitation evangelism—an organized canvass of a community in the interest of religion—has made a place for itself in the program of the church. But in general the churches open their doors Sunday mornings—and many of them Sunday mornings only—for worship, instruction and counsel. The service is one of dignity. It is primarily for those who consider themselves Christian and are within the church. Those who are without may be reached through personal contacts of one sort or another. This statement to be accurate must be explained. It represents a very notable trend, but applies mostly though not solely to churches that minister to the more educated classes. There are still numbers of churches that resent liturgical innovations and continue their informal and often crude practices.

It is education that has largely displaced evangelism. Here there has been an advance with unhappily incommensurate results. This shift in emphasis is probably caused by the increased sophistication of the religious community. It has been promoted by researches in child psychology and by the dissemination of information about the principles of pedagogy. Properly enough, the chief source of replenishment in the churches is the children whose parents are already members, supplemented by children whose parents have no particular religious interest, but are unwilling that their children should grow up without some religious instruction. The agent of religious education is primarily the Sunday School. The leading denominations in recent years have done excellently in preparation of material for it. The editors of periodicals for the Church School—a name superseding that of Sunday School in official, not in popular vocabularies—have been men and women trained in the science of pedagogy who have brought considerable ability to the selection of material and its application to the needs of children and youth. The record of the churches in this respect is deserving of great commendation. Not so much can be said for the teachers in the schools. The paucity of volunteers who are competent teachers has induced some churches that can afford it to resort to the dubious practice of paying trained teachers to take classes. That help can be obtained when pay is offered that will not be available for love is an uncomfortable fact. Most churches not opulent enough to pay their teachers must rely upon those who are willing quite apart from competence. The consequences are what might be expected. There are a few excellent teachers, the many are incompetent. Some realizing their lack of both knowledge and training commendably give their services rather than allow classes to be disbanded and children lost to the school. In general, the plain truth is that the churches are forced to take whom they can get for this most important work. In order to improve these conditions there have been training schools established in many communities for a few winter weeks where some, not all, take courses in Bible study and in teaching. Yet there is a vast contrast between the instruction in the weekday "public school" and that in the Sunday School. Of course the pupils are aware of it. In organization the churches have made a brave if imperfect effort to grade their schools after the fashion of the public schools. Aware of the deficiencies of the Sunday Schools there have been worked out plans to supplement them by means of weekday classes. These are usually interdenominational and are located in various sections of a city. The children of all the churches from that section attend the school in their part of town. Obviously small towns would be limited to one school for the whole community. That an hour a week on Sundays is insufficient time for adequate religious instruction is admitted. The chief weakness of the scheme described is that there is too often a failure to correlate the instruction of Sunday with that of the weekday. A child may be studying Old Testament stories on Sundays and the Life of Christ on Wednesday. It is rather confusing to the child. The churches have not decided with definiteness what is their purpose in religious education and what are the best means for accomplishing it. But America would be poor indeed without the religious education provided by the churches. Along with their regular and continual program for Christian teaching there has been a movement toward preparatory classes for adolescent children who are about to unite with the church. Here is a departure from old methods in the evangelical churches and the adoption of the plans long prevailing in the more liturgical churches. With it there is the implication that young people should come into the church through education rather than evangelization. When a child reaches the age of 12 or 14 it is taken for granted that he should become a member of the church. To be sure his assent is expected. But there is a change. Reliance is more upon education than evangelism or more accurately it is upon evangelism through education. Whatever the deficiencies—and a critical study cannot omit them—the churches merit honor for their earnest endeavors in religious education.

The Christian church has been interested in education in a broader way. Many of the great universities and colleges were founded as institutions of the church. In recent years these have been restive under church control, and there has been a peaceable secession that has reduced the number of educational institutions that are legally related to the denomination. They may retain in varying degrees their Christian heritage even without denominational affiliations. American educational history would be lacking indeed without the stimulus of the Christian churches.

The persistence of names designating homes for the needy and hospitals such as Saint John's Home or Presbyterian Hospital is a reminder of the pioneer service of the churches in respect of orphans, the sick and the poor. More and more are such institutions becoming the responsibility of the city rather than of private charity. But this does not vitiate the claim of the church to be the friend of the weak and suffering. A more modern adaptation of this service is to be seen in settlement-houses, community centers and "Americanization" projects. By no means can all of this beneficence be credited to organized religion. One of the earliest and most notable settlements, Hull House in Chicago with which the name of Jane Addams is associated, was not directly religious, but Miss Addams was a Christian and considered her work unlabeled Christianity in action.

The church had been accused of interest in the individual and not in society. The accusation never was true. There have been shifts in emphasis and widening of scope in Christian social action but never has it been excluded from the thought of the church. The hospitals alone refute the charge. Most of them were founded in the days of alleged individualism. Today, certainly, there can be no suspicion of Christian inertia in respect of social responsibilities. The leading denominations united to supplement and integrate their separate services in the Federal Council of the Churches of Christ in America. The Federal Council prepared the way for the National Christian Council that superseded it. The National Council, somewhat broader in scope and uniting additional denominational agencies in its co-operative plan, is essentially the same in principle as the Federal Council. In its brief history it has carried on in the work and spirit of its predecessor. This organization like the Federal Council which neither superseded nor controlled the denominations, contains a department of evangelism for co-operative campaigns to reach the individual, but its primary value is the combining of Protestant resources for social betterment. One mighty voice will command attention where many little voices will be ignored. Regiments formed into an army and thus all marching together may storm the city gates while straggling companies will be dispersed. For a recent Labor Sunday, the Federal Council sent out a message with the suggestion that it be read in all churches. It formulates six principles by which judgments and decisions may be made. They may be briefly summarized to demonstrate the role that Christian churches have assumed in trying to direct economic and political life in America to the halls of justice and the treasure house of good will. 1. "There should be a minimum standard of living to which every person has access." 2. "All persons have the moral right to equal opportunities to develop their capacities." 3. "Every able-bodied man and woman has the moral right and duty to serve the community in the home, through work under conditions that assure fair compensation, and in voluntary community service." 4. "Economic decisions are in large measure group decisions for which political forms of organization are necessary. The Christian's responsibility includes his taking a vigorous part in these political and economic activities which hold the greatest promise for the realization of Christian objectives. All persons have a moral right to such participation regardless of race, creed, color or sex." 5. "The churches have been right in giving encouragement to the development of the labor movement both as an instrument for the securing of greater economic justice and as a source of dignity

41

and morale for workers. Yet in specific issues that today may separate labor and management the church should not prejudge the rightness of either group. While judgments in particular cases should concentrate on the encouragement of all those processes which are in harmony with its ministry of reconciliation." 6. "Every national policy must be judged by its consequences for the lives of people in all lands and by its effects upon the economic basis for a peaceful world. There should be tolerance toward the economic experiments of other peoples though these must be judged by the same moral principles as our own."

This statement, primarily economic, indicates two other concerns of the church that have increasingly disturbed her conscience. One is racism the other is war. Psychologists and sociologists may probe for the roots of race prejudice, but we all know the sharp pain it inflicts and the injustices it creates. The relation of the negro to the white race is one of the distressing problems of our time. In all fairness we must admit it is a problem. Voluble denunciation of prejudice is easy. A prescription that is a theoretical panacea does not require an expert to write. There should be no race distinctions. All barriers should be leveled. All are children of God. This apparently would coincide with the New Testament teaching. But the solution is not so simple. Social living is complex. If the answers were all easy we should lack the discipline that life apparently is meant to subject us to. In our present world, can the welfare of man and what we call civilization best be advanced by the amalgamation of all races or by their continued separate existence with each contributing something unique from its culture for the good of all? We have now a most unhappy portion of our population of predominantly white blood but with enough negro blood to classify them as colored people. Are we willing that the American people should become a light brown or tawny white race? We are not willing; but should we be? In judging the southern people where race prejudice is strong and where segregation in spite of court decisions is insisted upon, we should recall the story of reconstruction days after the Civil War, when a fanatical, hating and unwise faction in the North controlled the Federal government and forced upon the South the rule of ignorant negroes who had just been released from slavery. Conditions became intolerable and the white population in defense of all that was good rose in more insidious and effective rebellion and saved their states from the corruption, aggrandizement, exploitation and downright wickedness inflicted upon them by illiterate negroes, white "carpet-baggers" and their rabid supporters in Washington. Southerners then vowed that they would never again submit to negro domination. It is against this background that judgment must be formed. We may not condone conditions, but we can understand them. Furthermore many in the South especially in the churches are changing their attitude toward the negro. They no longer favor the old kind of segregation. In the north where the problem is not absent but where the conditions are not acute it has been easy to be theoretically Christian and to pass resolutions condemning race prejudice. It requires no courage for a minister in whose church, located in a purely white neighborhood, there are no negroes to grow indignant at race injustices and to fulminate against them. For the church it should be written that promulgations from church assemblies and denunciations from pulpits are general and are quite sincere. Nor has it been mere talk. Where there have been conventions with delegates from both the races present there has usually been insistence that hotels should house and feed both races without discrimination. There are definite projects with the aim of cultivating mutual understanding and good will between the races. The New England minister who persuaded his congregation to accept a contingent of colored children as summer guests is a most striking illustration. In 1952 a white and a negro church in San Francisco united. It is more worthy of remark that in the South, Christian churches have taken the lead in a new approach to the negro question. Separation in religious gatherings there has been lessened though not abolished. The approach may be cautious, but it is Christian and most important it *is*! Southern churches in general are no longer content with the prevailing treatment of the negro nor complacent in the presence of the injustices to which he is forced to submit. Similarly there is Christian sensitiveness to unkind attitudes toward other races. Pronouncements, at least, upon racism are all that could be desired.

The case of the Jews in America is peculiar. The Jews are not a race according to ethnologists. Their distinctiveness is not really religious. The situation is unique in America. The distinctiveness of the religion of the Jews consists in the perpetuation of rites of a nation that has had no existence for nearly two thousand years. Even the new Jewish state is a conglomerate without either race or religious unity. They cherish the fiction of a non-existent race. Perhaps the best description of them has been that they constitute a kith. A multitude of them have lost all religion yet they continue to be Jews. Traits of character have been attributed to them that have made them unpopular. This is unfair because every person should be judged on his own merits. The underlying reason for suspicion of the Jew is that he alone in our white population is largely segregated. It may be partly because of prejudice against him that he feels excluded, but it is also because of his own insistence upon separation. And, if a generalization may be permitted the Jew is aggressive. The fanatical devotion of the majority of Jews in America to Zionism complicates the problem. The average citizen notwithstanding Jewish disclaimers cannot reconcile this apparent allegiance to a state in Palestine with full loyalty to the United

States. The explanation of sympathy for Jews without a country is scarcely satisfactory because the majority of displaced persons is not Jewish and the suffering of some of these is comparable to that inflicted upon the Jews. From a reading of Jewish pronouncements one gets the impression that the Jew is interested solely in the plight of the Jew. Others than Jews are concerned about displaced persons as such—Jews and Gentiles. It is scarcely singular then that human nature being what it is there should be considerable anti-Semitism in the land. It is just superficial to make a declaration either of Christian opinion or conduct. Even right-thinking people are puzzled and uneasy especially as the politicians with their keen scent for blocs of votes make matters worse by accentuating differences while with pious gusto they decry them. Anti-Semitism is anti-Christian. There can be no argument about that. But the problem cannot be brushed away with a few homilies on the un-Christian character of racism. What the church has done has been to make straightforward declarations condemnatory of race prejudice. There is Christian preaching to the Jews, but the increasing tendency of churches is to blur if not erase the line separating Judaism and Christianity—rabbis are members of ministerial associations. There is an occasional exchange of pulpits between rabbis and ministers and there are from time to time union services of synagogue and church. And from nearly every Christian pulpit there has been courage in urging good will toward the Jews upon congregations that were not always conspicuous for such good will. In truth there must be a distinction between the formal position of the church and the actual feeling of many Christian people.

Indisputably the Christian must cultivate good will toward Jews and kindly relations with them. In their practical dealings individual Christians are often suspicious. It is understandable though not justifiable. A Christian citizen and Christian business man may conscientiously ask what his practical relation should be. Is he justified from what he considers conclusive experience in being extra cautious in dealing with Jews in business? It would be utterly false to assert that Jews universally subordinate in their loyalty America to Palestine but, denials notwithstanding, a large number of Jews talk and act that way. The conclusion may not be entirely fair but it does look to many Gentiles like a double allegiance. As a citizen how shall the Christian act politically toward those who he believes subordinate America to Palestine? Such are the practical difficulties. If the church has failed in erasing suspicion of the Jew among the people it has not been wholly because of prejudice. But there is prejudice enough.

To the credit of the church, it should be said that there is real progress in creating a thoroughly Christian attitude not only toward Jews but toward the foreigners from many lands who dwell among us. It is far from perfection but the Christian churches constitute the greatest influence in abolishing the prejudice of race.

It is the conviction of some that Christian principles are perfectly plain. All that we need to do is to formulate them and put them into practice. These good people are honestly amazed that there should be both discussion and dissent. What they fail to see and will not believe is that in our world of relatives, not absolutes, principles may be in conflict with each other, in a war-ridden world. This is nowhere more evident than in the quest for peace. Is it not Christian teaching that men and nations should live in peace with each other? There can be no doubt of it. Then in the name of logic and religion why not denounce all wars and refuse to have part in any? To this the reply is made that the enslavement of peoples, national sadism are also contrary to Christian principles and we must choose between adherence to an un-Christian peace that actually means hatred, conflict and destruction of the weak, or engage in a war to halt an aggressor. The position of the Church should be judged in the light of these honest differences of conviction. It is difficult to obtain a unanimous statement about peace and war from any church assembly unless it is vague. The Church has submitted to wars it regarded as unavoidable while at the same time it condemned war as irrational and un-Christian. With these differences in mind we may proceed to a consideration of the influence of the church for peace. This has been chiefly exercised in two ways. The first is through constant reiteration of the wickedness and folly of war and the rightness and wisdom of peace. Experience has aided Christian teaching here. We are disillusioned about the benefits of war even to the victors. There are only a few obstinate militarists who really believe in war these days. There remains a reluctant acquiescence in the belief that the possibility of a war that must be fought to avoid a still greater evil cannot be denied. But this realization stimulates to more zeal in promoting the ideals of peace. The American churches are reaching friendly hands across the seas to Christians in other lands that brotherhood may be emphasized and that the churches of the world may be one in efforts for peace. The church is thus definitely engaged in a campaign for peace. The second way by which the church has given itself to the achievement of peace is through what we might call the practice of Christian statesmanship. This entails the meeting of concrete and specific circumstances for the development of international good feeling. The churches press the government to use all reasonable means for reaching international understanding. It deprecates war-hysteria that is so easily aroused. It enters into relations with churches of other lands so that common projects may draw nations together. European churches destroyed by the war have been rebuilt by American money. A definite organization "Church World Service" has been organized. Its mission is set forth in its name. Packages to the destitute and suffering have crossed the Atlantic to bear practical demonstration of Christian sympathy to those who have known the devastation of war. The church has no cause for shame with such a record. The Church of the Prince of Peace has not defaulted.

One of the most conspicuous entrances for the church into national political order for social well-being is its long campaign for temperance. So persistent has been this campaign that the very word temperance has acquired a restricted meaning as ordinarily used. Nobody needs to be told that a temperance movement is one against alcohol. The particular sin of drunkenness has been selected as the social enemy number one. That the attack on the liquor traffic has often been made most intemperately is a rather amazing and confusing illustration of the narrowing of the word temperance to the one application of alcoholic indulgence. A further interesting metamorphosis of the word temperance is that as used in this war against liquor it does not mean temperate drinking, but total abstinence.

The reasons for all this arise from the realization of the incalculable social evil of drunkenness. Liquor has ruined lives, wrecked homes, corrupted government. Interest in abolishing this egregious sin has not been impersonal. Too many women had seen how liquor had changed their husbands from decent men into brutes, how savings dwindled and earnings were squandered and life was demoralized. It is no wonder that indignation became anger and anger often flamed into fanaticism. Makers and sellers of liquor became powerful forces in the politics of cities. They often controlled mayors and city councils. Christian people were outraged. Through one means and another they kept the war going against the liquor interests until in an avalanche of protest they crushed their enemy and outlawed traffic in liquor through a constitutional amendment. It is contended

48

that emotions outran judgment. Conditions under the 18th amendment were notoriously bad. Bootleggers were everywhere. The law was openly flouted. Probably the effect of the amendment was to decrease somewhat the consumption of liquor. It was more expensive and the poor could not obtain it as easily as in the old days. But the rich were not deterred by law. Since there was no regulation, liquor was concocted of various ingredients that did not render it less dangerous. Certainly what was gained in the decrease of drinking was lost in the prevalence of lawlessness. The plain truth—hard for many to accept—is that a law to be effective must be supported by overwhelming public sentiment.

The 18th amendment has been repealed. Liquor is back; it has brought its old evils with it. Whether total abstinence, temperance in the original meaning of the word, closer government regulation, prohibition of the so-called hard liquors only or some other method is the object for which the people of the churches should strive is still a question in dispute. All Christian people were not and are not prohibitionists, but the majority in the churches in favor of outlawing liquor was so large that this can be considered a major, possibly *the* major attempt of the church to wrestle with a recognized social evil. Opinions will continue to differ about the wisdom and justice of prohibition and the effectiveness of the methods sought by the churches to gain their objective, but there can be no difference of opinion about the financial, moral, spiritual toll exacted from the country by drunkenness, made worse in these days of the motor car, or of the high motives and the zeal of the churches in their undaunted determination to do something toward social reconstruction through abolition or control of the traffic in liquor.

In appraising the worth of the Protestant churches of America a high place should be given to magnificent intangible idealism. The country has gone through vicissitudes of

prosperity with the dangers of materialism, of adversity with
its temptation to surrender the good as not worth the effort
to obtain or retain, it has known war with its hatred and its
tragedies, peace with its temptation to complacency and
selfish individualism, it has been blighted by a frost of
unbelief and lulled into false optimism by sporadic revivals
of faith, it has listened to the cold views of a naturalistic
science and has been scorched by the heat of industrial conflict, but throughout all the church of Jesus Christ has held
before the eyes of men a cross of forgiveness, sacrifice and
love. In the midst of the worst materialistic time the church
has presented the priority of the spiritual, in days of the
ascendancy of the secular it has urged the claims of the
spiritual, against the arrogant claims of atheistic science it
has asserted the realities of Christian experience, when class
has fought class, it has preached the ideals of brotherhood.
There have been many practical failures, no doubt. The
church at times has yielded to temptations of pride and
power. But ever has the church proclaimed its ideals to the
people of this land. Certainly there is no institution that
compares with the church in upholding standards of goodness and kindness. This is not only past history, it is present
practice.

The church has been a fortress against the assaults of
secularism and an aggressive army in attacking this modern
enemy. At times there has been—indeed there still continues
—a disposition to divide life into two areas, the sacred and
the secular. Life cannot be so divided. To the consternation
of Christian people the recognition of the impossibility of
that kind of division has not resulted as was hoped in the
sanctification of all life, but in its secularization. By many
this is regarded as the chief enemy of religion and indeed of
humanity in our day. The course to be pursued by religion
was clear. That all life should be brought under the direction of God, that the kingdom of heaven comprehends the

50

whole of life is a conception not just implicit in the teaching of the New Testament but explicit in its principles and their application. Accordingly one of the most wholesome impacts of the Christian pulpit upon contemporary life is its reiterated insistence that industry, so important in our world today and so prominent in social thinking, should be organized and directed by Christian principles. The noticeable change in attitude in many—not all by any means—industrialists is partly in response to the urging of our social prophets. That the public need not be considered, that working people are just "hands" is no longer a popular doctrine. Executives in business are increasingly given to a feeling that something is owed to the public and few would dare openly to avow the belief that management has no duty to consider the welfare of its workers as human beings with families to support and entitled to a share in the opportunities supposed to be offered universally in democratic America. Management has sat in pews and listened to the reiteration of these truths, has gone out and reflected upon this practical application of Christianity and has induced action, too. This interpretation of Christianity is not limited to a lesson in business relations but includes our pleasures and in fact all phases of life. Against secularism, the church urges the demands of the Kingdom of God that all things shall be made sacred.

The contact of great men with the church often constitutes an impact of the church upon the world. The names of certain scientists of highest rank who are also confessed Christians will occur to the reader. It is illuminating to know that these men took with them to laboratory or observatory a genuine and first hand Christian experience. They accepted with scientific impartiality all the results of experiment and observation, but they also were in possession of an inner light which could not be put out. So the church has set before the nation scientists who found no incompatibility between their researches and their religious faith. This has been a gift worth counting. Along with scientists the church has developed Christian scholars who in various fields of learning have enlarged our spiritual horizons and enriched our religious understanding. To the Christians if not to the world the knowledge of the Scriptures through the conflation of manuscripts with the consequent revision has been a boon indeed. The study of comparative religion has given a new and helpful perspective. Since there is no real line of demarcation between areas of knowledge the researches of scholars in the fields of Christian thought are likewise contributions to the general understanding. A scholar whose approach to the study of the period of the Protestant Reformation is that of Christian interest nevertheless may add to the understanding of the period by historians who care nothing about the religious issues involved.

Greater than the production of Christian scholars is the production of saints. We use the word in its popular meaning of men of superior character, spiritual discernment, who have abounded in good work. There are men and women of prominence, known to all the Christian community, who are recognized as saintly. Their influence has been strong. Names need not be mentioned. But how many quiet, humble unknown Christians have so exemplified the spirit of their Lord that they have merited the recognition of superior worth! Here is a man who was a machinist. He had only a rudimentary education. He had been reared in a Christian home that was narrow in its sectarianism. As a young man he became indifferent to religion. Dissatisfied with this kind of life, he sought the church to discover whether or not it could supply the help he needed. There was no mistaking his earnestness when he was received into the church. There his transparent sincerity and his faithfulness earned him an office of spiritual importance. He re-

52

garded the responsibilities of that office seriously. His public prayers almost as if by a miracle were not so ungrammatical as his ordinary conversation. And they were prayers. They were simple, well-worded, earnest. Those who heard them felt that they reached the throne of grace. He was neither afraid nor ashamed to talk his religion in the shop, but there was no intrusiveness in it and it was not sanctimonious. He was true to his convictions. Others about him might betray their weakness in yielding to expediency. Lower considerations might motivate them. They might display a spirit that was hardly Christian. Not so with him: Loyal, courageous, even outspoken, his life was Christlike. Nobody knows how many there are like this humble saint—who would be astonished at the designation—but in most churches there are a few superior souls whose lives are centers of divine radiation. They live and die unsung. Many are humble and obscure, but in evaluating the church they must not be forgotten.

We draw near to a church building—something concrete —stone, brick or wood to be sure. It may be an architectural monstrosity, an edifice that awakens derision or disgust. It may be modernistic with the utilitarian concept prominent in its form and arrangement. But often it is beautiful, exhibiting qualities associated with the church throughout the ages and possessing a form that is not only appropriate to its spirit, but an expression of it. Such are the lovely churches—some of them small and simple—that help endear New England to the visitor as well as to the native born. Such, too, are certain of the magnificent city churches such as Riverside Church in New York or the even larger neighboring cathedral. That religion has given to the nation edifices that lift up the souls of men, that seem to have caught and held the beauty of holiness, is something that no fair-minded person would discount.

We enter the church. The organ, the instrument that seems to have borrowed its tone from heaven for worship upon earth, greets us with its melody. The pulpit with its great Bible or perchance a cross is in the center of our vision. Here is a reminder of the gospel to which the church owes its existence. We take our seats. Hymns are sung, the Scripture is read, prayer is offered, a sermon is preached. In all there are possibilities of helpfulness. A sinner smitten by his conscience may find peace through the proclamation of God's pardon. A mind that is filled with perplexities may know the dawn of inner light. A soul forced to make decisions but unable to bring itself to their making may become conscious of new strength. A lonely spirit may be introduced to the Spirit of Jesus the comrade of those who walk the ways of solitude. The weary, faltering and almost fainting, may hear a voice saying "Come unto me and I will give you rest," believe the word and go forth refreshed. One who is tortured by sorrow may discover comfort that sustains. This ministry of the church is measured by no rule, weighed by no scales. Could there be anything grander? To lead impoverished souls to the treasury of grace, to commit the defeated to an invincible captain, to open the gates of a garden to those who live in desert places, surely nothing can surpass this ministry of the Christian church.

There is that in the human spirit that craves something beyond itself—something higher, finer, more enduring. There is an intuition, it may be, that the curtain that separates man from this higher world is not impenetrable. With crudeness, superstition, folly and even wickedness men have attempted to rend that veil. But in its more enlightened and purer forms this faith in the immortal partakes of the spirit of worship. The church of the gospel of Jesus invites men to worship the highest that is known to man.

When we think of what has been done to foster this

54

approach to God we consider not only sermons and symbols, but the songs of faith. Music has a unique office in life. In Christian worship music may be united with intelligent and inspiring sentiment. If we are to appraise the value of the church we must mention the hymns that have enriched worship and by their poetry have glided into the spirits of worshipers. Even if we confine ourselves to hymns of American writers there is a list which we cherish. Oliver Wendell Holmes' hymn "Lord of all being throned afar" should stand near the front in worthfulness. There are the two familiar hymns of Whittier "We may not climb the heavenly steeps to bring the Lord Christ down" and "Dear Lord and Father of mankind, forgive our feverish ways." Still more modern are Washington Gladden's beautiful stanzas, "O Master let me walk with thee, in lonely paths of service free" and more recent, is Frank Mason North's "Where cross the crowded ways of life." What has the church done for America? It has given these hymns that have lifted up men's hearts, inspired their actions and confirmed their faith.

The visitor who explores beyond the sanctuary of the modern church will discover numerous rooms adapted to a variety of purposes. There will be assembly rooms and class rooms for religious education. They will be equipped with blackboards, sand piles, maps, charts, books. This is to be expected in a church that takes seriously the task of education in religion. But these rooms or other rooms will also be the meeting-place for various organizations, boy scouts for example. It will be observed that the churches are giving opportunities for the social life of their people, especially of their youth. There is a sincere attempt to furnish young men and young women with these social activities in a Christian atmosphere. There may even be a gymnasium or, at least, a place for basket ball. The churches have taken responsibility for the full development of the boys and girls under their influence. Even beyond this there is often provision made for those in the community who are outside of the church for the churches feel a responsibility for their communities too. There is the vacation school where boys and girls from the neighborhood are invited to work, play, study and learn practical religion in sharing not only with each other but with children in other lands.

One of the chief benefits conferred by American Protestantism upon the United States has been its espousal of liberty. For the most part the colonies were not noted for religious tolerance. Roger Williams exiled from Massachusetts because of his religious beliefs founded in Providence the first government in history absolutely dedicated to liberty of conscience. It was Williams who planted the seed. It grew slowly, but it grew. When the first ten amendments to the constitution were adopted—those amendments that are called "The Bill of Rights"—it was largely because of the influences of churches especially in Virginia. Cognate with liberty is democracy. These twins have ever been under the watchful eye and fostering care of the Christian people. In our day the foremost champions of liberty and democracy are by no means all people of the churches. Yet there is no institutional segment of our nation that is more committed to the maintenance of liberty and the promotion of democracy than the churches.

Even a brief survey of what the churches are and of what they do reveals them as indispensable to the welfare of the community. Their light has not gone out. Many of the benefits conferred are plain, indeed inescapable, many are intangible, but none the less real. These are beautiful, spiritual tapestries woven with invisible threads. The town without a church is poor indeed. It is conceded generally that in an inventory of the worth in a tiny village or a huge city the possession of churches would have considerable to do with entitling it to a high rating. The church is not ideal, but it may properly be idealized. The city built upon the hill cannot be hidden. Thus stands the church commanding attention as it endures upon its rocky height, viewing the past and the future and devoted to the present.

Chapter III

THE DEFECTS OF THE CHURCH

Any objective, fair-minded discussion of the Christian church must acclaim the glory of its principles and the magnificent record of its achievements, but the same impartiality will disclose all that is faded and all that is false—and there is the faded and there is the false.

The chief counts in the indictment brought by criticism against the church are three in number and more than numerically devastating in their implications of guilt. The three counts are worldliness, unbrotherliness and indifference. The very nature of these sins tends to make the perpetrators unaware of their committal. They go along blithely unconscious of their betrayal of that which is most distinctive in the religion they profess. Such accusations supported by evidence, if they do not strike at the root of the tree, certainly lop off prominent if unhealthy branches and denude it of conspicuous if artificial foliage. Reduced to reality, the church to some will have a somewhat scraggly appearance.

We must consider these criticisms in order and in detail. First there must be explanation if not technical definition. What is meant by "worldliness?" A generation or two ago certain practices like dancing, card-playing and theatergoing were singled out and labeled "worldly." More mature consideration has shown that these distinctions were not only inadequate but unreal. Nowadays Christians of the finest attainment may be seen on the floor of the ballroom, and at the card table. Nor do they feel it necessary to justify their support of so noble an art as that of the drama. It was a matter of observation, too, that men who refrained from those amusements on religious grounds were not always scrupulous in their business dealings, considerate of those who worked for them, or averse to the practices of aggrandizement. A new definition was in order. It is not to say that either the church or its critics without, consciously formulated a definition. Indeed, the word worldliness was loosely used to express an idea and a feeling that because it was vague and unreal made the churchman uncomfortable and furnished ammunition for those who would attack the institution. However, everyone must admit that it is fundamental to the church to build upon eternal principles. There would be no reason for its existence if it did not believe in a kingdom of God that transcends earthly time. The rupture between God and man is caused by the human insistence upon the priority of the physical and the temporal with a consequent disregard of the realm of the spirit. Christianity teaches the primacy of truth and goodness and their eternal value. He who has no religious outlook lives as if life had its complete meaning here and now. Consequently he will equate life's values with present possessions and attainments. If there is no meaning beyond the transitory it is hard to avoid the ambition to accumulate money, indulge in pleasure and strive for popular success. He who thus lives as if life had no meaning beyond this world and its conventions is worldly. It is in such fashion that we reckon worth in dollars—"How much is he worth?"—success in "getting ahead"—the implication is "ahead of others," a good time in indulgence—we note the use of "good." When the standards of living are these we have perfect evidence of what worldliness means. In contrast is the life of the spirit. Here the dominant purpose is to use money to advance truth and to help mankind, the ambition is not competition in order to get ahead, but co-operation and service. Pleasure becomes a means for re-creation. Character assumes primary importance.

This attitude is not the assumption of "other-worldliness" in the sense that men should be exhorted to submit to removable evils of the present in expectation of compensation for their sufferings, in a world to come. It is other-worldliness only in its expression of faith in an eternal order, its denial that causes and effects are to be computed only by transient standards, that this earth with its history is the sole stage for the drama of mankind and that the interpretation of life must be confined to its narrow boundaries.

Therefore there is no contradiction in the present emphasis upon the social application of Christian principles. In fact it is the failure to make such application that in part constitutes the worldliness of the church.

It has already been indicated that the pulpit is not silent upon the fundamental iniquity of unjust and unsympathetic social attitudes nor do church assemblies fail to express disapproval. The World Council of Churches meeting for the first time in Amsterdam was vocal upon these issues. At the same time the failure of the local church to apply these principles has been lamentable and conspicuous. Color lines are drawn, social inequities are condoned because the local church relegates such matters to the periphery of its interests while it concentrates attention and effort upon quite other concerns. Admittedly there is sometimes a concentration upon individualism because of a very restricted theology. Ritual may assume exclusive importance. Preachers aware of the futility of attacks upon social wrongs, may sometimes feel that the sole result of their exhortations is to draw the fire of angry parishioners upon themselves. Even though the preachers are brave and conscientious they will discover that much of their message is futile in respect of the congregation to which it is especially addressed. There may be a general and distant interest in these goals of the gospel, but the immediate interest is elsewhere. This substitution of prevalent standards for those of the gospels constitutes the worldliness justly attributed to the church today.

We must be still more specific. This would involve a long recital to be complete, but even a few illustrations will make the meaning clear.

The theoretical interest of the church as set forth in the Bible and expounded in the pulpit is the spiritual welfare and advancement of men. No doubt there is this interest. Practically, however, the chief interest of the church is to build an effective organization. Effective for what? The quick answer is for this spiritual welfare and advancement of men. But the quick answer is not accurate. We must consider more carefully. Our age is one that has perfected organization. There has been genius in this. Governments have become complicated. They have become so complicated that often they seem tied tight with red tape. But the marvel really is that such cumbersome collections of bureaus, departments, various administrative units all inter-related and having a degree of unification can function at all. Business has become big. Here again the complexities of organization are almost beyond understanding. The stock exchange with its trading facilities for hundreds of diverse stocks, the banks with their method of inter-change through a clearing-house, all add up to an amazing total of organizational genius in business. Even education is no longer the simple device of a log with Mark Hopkins on one end and a student on the other. The universities enroll students by the thousand and tens of thousands. The President of the university is no longer a clergyman or an educator, but an executive. It is interesting to note this evolution. First as education was closely affiliated with religion of which knowledge was the handmaiden, the ideal was the development of scholarship with the implication that it was essential to a

Christianity that was devoted to truth. Then, with the advancement of psychological pedagogy, emphasis shifted. The head of an institution of learning it was thought should be one who understood the principles of education. The clergyman as college president was relegated to antiquity. Education must be more independent of religion. Ties that bound colleges to denominations were cut with cheer, not with regret. Interest in education widened. More and more youth went to college. The colleges, eager for more students and reflecting the practical trend in the conception of life, broadened their curricula to include more and more vocational courses. The natural result has been expansion. More buildings, more equipment, more money were required. Hence the president of the university or college must be the man with business ability who not only can administer a great institution but can raise money to keep pace with its increasing needs, and this conception now largely dominates even church colleges.

Such is the background of the Christian church in the world in which we live. Undoubtedly the Spirit of God can use executive talents as well as talents of teaching or evangelism. Undoubtedly an organization can be the vehicle through which that Spirit can promote the interests of the divine kingdom. It has indeed been necessary to build up organization in our world that is no longer simple in its social or economic structure. Hence not only have the denominations developed more and more synods, conferences, associations, assemblies, conventions, but there has been differentiation of work through departments and societies for foreign missions, home missions, education, publication and the various other forms of modern service. Similarly, the churches are organized. There are boards, committees, projects, schools, campaigns. Although there may be and very often is over-organization, the demands of the time have sanctioned this institutional growth. But it is attended with dangers. Once again the alleged end is largely lost in the exaltation of the means until the means becomes the end in itself. Organization for its own sake as a matter of pride, as a standard of judgment and a demonstration of success becomes the objective of endeavor. This can be illustrated on the higher levels of missionary and philanthropic service through interdenominational organization. A few years ago there was a worthy and necessary work of mercy undertaken by such a means. Appeals were made to the churches and the responses in giving were generous. It was announced that one more appeal would be made. After that since the work that called the organization into being was completed, the books would be closed and the organization dissolved. The appeal was made, the churches again made their contributions of money. Then what happened? Secretaries of the organization appeared before ministerial groups asking for the perpetuation of the organization. They were often heard with amazement. The work was in its nature temporary, the need had been rather well met. But other work could be done it was explained. In a world that lacks so much, obviously anyone could find something more to do, but it was apparent that representatives of the work were loath to surrender their positions and allow the organization to be discontinued. In some instances, at least, the request was flatly and decisively rejected. But the organization continued, changing its name slightly and continues to this day. It has probably done much good, but its continuance was patently for reasons rather selfish.

On the level of the individual church the pre-eminence of organization as an end in itself is astonishing. What are the criteria of a "successful" church? They are largely statistical. How large is its membership? Often you hear the boast that a certain church is the largest in the city, in the denomination or in the country. How many new members have been received during the previous year? How many have come into the church through confession of faith? How much money has been raised? Are the congregations increasing or decreasing? Is the church well organized? The year book of the denominations reports these statistics. The denominational paper applauds the church that has had a "phenomenal growth" and deplores the churches that had few or no accessions during the year. It often is true that a little country church struggling for its very existence in a diminishing community deserves far more credit though its statistical columns record zeros than a big city church with its large budget, modern facilities and growing neighborhood that has added hundreds to its roll. In the denomination recognition and preferment are given to the "important" church and its "important" minister.

In contrast items might be taken from the diary of many a minister that would have a similar reading and connotation. The telephone rings. The minister answers. He recognizes the voice of a woman not a member of his church. It is an agitated voice that speaks. "Can you go to see my daughter? I think she will listen to you and maybe you can do something with her. She needs someone to advise and help her in her family difficulties." The minister goes to the home of the daughter, learns the circumstances that have brought trouble and threaten disaster, tries to calm and to counsel. When he leaves the home the family is more hopeful of a solution of difficulties. All agree to try to work things out.

The minister learns of a woman incurably ill in a hospital. She is not a member of his church. Her name will never be added to its roll, but she is ill and needs comfort and faith although she does not know that her illness is fatal. He goes to the hospital, knocks on the door of the patient's room, is bidden to enter. He enters and the sick woman greets him cordially. "I was sure that if you knew I were ill you would come to see me." He sits by her bedside, tries to bring her cheer and commends the God and Father of Jesus Christ to her. She is grateful for all. It is the beginning of a quiet ministry that ends only when the life of the woman goes out.

There is a summons for the minister to go to a house of mourning. He goes. He conducts a service over the form of the dear one who has gone. He tries to bring consolation to hurt lives, to interpret griefs in terms of a God who loves. He is richly repaid by the evidence that his service has helped. But the family does not belong to his church and probably never will.

A young man comes to the minister's study. The youth has his own problems. They are problems incidental to his expanding knowledge as he wrestles with questions arising in his college experience. He does not understand. His religion may be in peril. Related to these are problems of living. Decisions must be made but first of all issues must be clarified. The minister listens understandingly, sympathetically. Those problems are not necessarily alien to his experience. He, too, went to college and was confronted with similar dilemmas. From his own experience he is in a position to help his young inquirer. He gives him clues of interpretation. He makes clearer the issues. He eases the mental and spiritual tension. The young man goes away braced up. Upon graduation from college the young man may move into another community and be lost to the particular church for which the minister is responsible.

Of none of these ministries is the church ever aware. They are quiet, confidential matters that are not announced from the pulpit. None of them adds the slightest to the strength of the ecclesiastical organization. No names are added to the roll through them, no subscriptions are made for the financial benefit of the institution because of them. The congregation is not increased by a single attendant through such ministries. Instead these calls upon the pastor of a

church will take considerable time that otherwise might be devoted to building up the organization. But what Christian who had not the spirit of an Esau would hesitate in evaluating these services as the very essence of Christian discipleship? Are not these quiet, almost hidden ministries the real assets of a Christian church? They are not so regarded by the average church. Words of approval might be spoken of them. Practically they are left out of computation of the worth of the church and its ministry. If this sort of service results as it sometimes does in visible effects, such as bringing new members into the church, it is hailed as an achievement. There are many ministers, however, counted successful because they have recorded accessions to their churches and have gained financial progress who would unhesitatingly acknowledge that their greatest achievements and most satisfactory were those that did not appear in church records. To bring comfort to the afflicted, hope and faith to sinners, strength to the faltering, purpose to the frustrated, is to serve Jesus Christ. This perhaps should be, but is not, synonymous with the work of the church. Even of a Sunday morning the worth of the service is not to be measured by the size of the congregation, the "popular appeal" of the preacher, the number of accessions, the amount of the collection, but by the people who were helped, by those who go from the house of God with fresh courage to face the week, those who carry home with them something that will stay with them during the days to come. There is surely no inconsistency between helping people on the one hand and having large congregations, eloquent preaching and many accessions on the other. But the two do not invariably go together and the standard of judgment is almost always the tangible, the visible, that which can be counted, the organizationally desirable. And that is the standard of the world.

Then there must be organizations within the organization. "Is the church well organized?" is a usual question. A bustling, hustling institution that shows results in the columns of figures is the generally accepted description of the successful church. Such a church may indeed be successful in the highest sense, but this does not necessarily follow. There is an American delight in "a going concern," a pride in belonging to a society that ranks well in the estimation of the community. It should be admitted that there is probably no church where there are not at least some members who do not mistake realities in this way. Motives are mixed. But practically—not in theory to be sure—the purpose in the churches is to build up an institution successful according to current standards, trimmed with pious decorations. To how large an extent these conceptions prevail is open to debate. That they prevail is indisputable.

In business, competition is expected. It may be considered necessary for the preservation of free enterprise. The churches have taken over the idea. They are as ruthless as business. The Christian ideal is quite contrary. The strong are to bear the burdens of the weak. Co-operation is the Christian principle. This is recognized and is sometimes practiced. In foreign missions work there is an interdenominational comity that allots areas to denominations. If a given area is allotted to one denomination, others are in honor bound to keep out and to avoid duplication in a world that is so vast there is not only room but need for all the missioners of Christianity that can be sent out and maintained. In the United States there have been notable and commendable efforts to abolish competition between churches in small villages. Community or federated churches have been established with much benefit to all. Occasionally, at least, this has been the result of idealism upon the part of denominational or local leaders who have deprecated the waste of energy incidental to division. They have felt it was most worthy to get Christians to worship together. Often the union has been of necessity. Two or three churches in a community barely able to support one have been struggling for breath and the only chance of survival has been through union. Sometimes one of several village churches is really alive and the others are barely existing. The weaker ones will unite or federate with the one that is not hopelessly on the decline, save themselves and serve the community.

With all this accomplished it is still true that in many small settlements churches compete with each other in a struggle for survival that is quite as ruthless as that predicated by Darwin in his "Origin of Species." In the cities competition is quite as acute. It is not only interdenominational. It is within a denomination. Let a new family arrive in a town or in a neighborhood and immediately it is besieged by ministers and members of the churches that have any hope of securing the allegiance of the newcomers. Often the siege is hard-pressed. Arguments are waged, inducements, usually social, are offered to secure new members. If the new family is one of strong denominational loyalty—unusual today—it is only with great reluctance that the churches of another name will relinquish their intended victim to be fought over by the several churches in the denomination to which the new people are inextricably attached. It is not uncommon to learn that some over-zealous minister has written to another church for letters of dismissal for a family without the formality of obtaining the consent of the family. There is an amusing story—if such stories can be amusing—and said to be true—of two churches in a village of several thousand that united in an evangelistic campaign. Knowing the predatory propensities of the ministers and churches involved it was agreed beforehand that if there were any converts as the result of the union meetings they should be allowed to choose the church they would join voluntarily and without influence being exerted upon them. After several days there was a convert.

The Reverend Mr. A., pastor of one of the churches, apparently argued himself into the belief that he had made an unholy agreement with his fellow minister when he had consented not to influence any converts. In any event he somehow justified himself into calling upon the man converted to invite the convert to join his church. He went to the home of the convert and was admitted to the living room where he found the Reverend Mr. B., pastor of the other church bent upon securing a new member for his church. The story has two points that are stimulating to reflection. First the two ministers involved were good, not bad men, even though in that instance they may have acted badly. They were both sincere and earnest men who were under compulsion to bring into their churches every possible member. Secondly the people in the town who were not in any church told the story with great glee. A young physician and his family moved into a small city. A church in the neighborhood was so aggressive in its attempts to gain the physician and his wife as members that he was disgusted and for that reason refused to join that church. To anyone with experience, these are commonplace matters. The keen and continuous competition is not limited to attempts to reach newcomers, but sometimes shows itself in an attempt to wrench members from other local churches. Ministers have been known to call on members of other churches and indulge freely in criticism of those churches and their ministers with whose theology, perchance, they may not have agreed. There are ministers who are embodiments of courtesy, who are generous and unselfish, who are scrupulous in their dealings and resist the pressure put upon them to enter into ungodly competition. But even they are forced to compete. It is the way of the churches. Competition may be on higher levels with a refusal to stoop to that which is rankly offensive to one of fine spirit, but if the organization is to be maintained it will be by competition.

The writer in his first pastorate was rather startled by the remark of a business woman, a real Christian and faithful to her church to the effect that she would rather deal with business people than with churches. She believed the business people were more scrupulous. It is to be hoped her opinion was wrong, but that it could come from the experience of a fine Christian spirit is itself startling.

If the whole community were Christian and church-going all the churches might be filled, although whether or not it would be economical and spiritually wise to have so many separate churches is a question. As conditions are there are certainly not enough people with Christian interest to fill half of them—except on Easter Sunday. If a church is to prosper it must enter into competition with other churches to get the people. It is the essence of worldliness.

The churches copy the world in their social distinctions, although they make a brave attempt to appear innocent. It is not true as it is frequently alleged that the laboring class has lost interest in the church, that is it is not true of laboring people particularly. All classes of the social order show little interest in the church. The rich are spending Sundays on their yachts or at cocktail parties, in their cars or on golf links. The middle class according to its means is following the rich. The working man is driving his car, listening to the radio, working in his garden, attending the neighborhood picture theater. But some of the rich are in church. So are some of the middle class. So are some of the laboring people. In many cities half of the churches are composed largely of those who work with their hands. It is true of Baptist and Methodist churches, to a less extent of Presbyterian and Congregational churches and to a still less extent of Episcopal churches. This leaves out Nazarenes, the Church of God, and similar smaller sects that are nearly confined to the uneducated masses. Nevertheless class distinctions differ little within church walls from class distinctions without church walls. In a church of the socially elite there will not be many from poor neighborhoods. The big business man, his wife and family, the professional man, his wife and family, will not often be found in a church of the common people. The classes mix in church only a little better than they do in worldly institutions. A poorly dressed man who entered a church of the rich would probably be courteously received and shown to a pew. But he would be unlikely to enter even for one service. It is true that people naturally find their own level even in churches, but religion is not the determinant there. The rustle of silk and the flash of a diamond pendant make as much of an impression in the aisle of the house of God as on the promenade of Vanity Fair. In the average church there is hesitancy mounting to fear lest some action may alienate the rich and influential. "He is a good giver and we can't afford to offend him" is the opinion of the Board, ratified by the congregation. In a rich city church the minister asked a socially prominent woman of the congregation to call upon a newcomer. The request was considered in a desire to be obliging and to discharge a possibly Christian duty, then declined. Why? Because, explained the society woman, if she called it would be tantamount to placing the name of the newcomer upon her social list and, of course, such a misunderstanding must be avoided. Is this Christianity — or worldliness?

Music ministers to the spiritual needs of many people. It is quite right that organist, choir and congregation should keep on the key and not commit musical mayhem upon the composition rendered. Therefore standards of music are high—musically. The volunteer choir is not always an eminent artistic success. It is tolerated of necessity for the reason that the church cannot afford better music. It costs money. But in accordance with its financial ability a church improves its musical programme. A proficient organist is engaged, a quartette displaces or leads the volunteer choir, a capable director teaches the less trained singers. He can always fall back on his quartette or select one as a soloist. Music is a drawing-card in churches. Members who have little religious interest will go to a church for its music. At Easter the churches vie with each other in presenting great programmes of music—sometimes a great programme of great music. Surely the best music is none too good for the Lord God! But the prerequisites in engaging organists and singers are usually entirely musical. Religious requirements are secondary if indeed they exist at all. What can an organist applying for a position in a church offer as qualifications? If he is a member of the guild of organists it is evident that he is musically capable. If such credentials are not forthcoming ability and experience elsewhere are examined by the music committee. It is to be expected that he has a proper reputation as a man and a citizen. He may be an atheist. If his atheism is not too blatant there will probably be no questions asked. A singer steps into the choir loft and gives a sample of her vocal ability. Upon that she is judged. Nobody inquires about her Christian attitude. She may be a devoted believer whose chief ambition is to use her gifts for the help of others—which is to the Glory of God. She may be a casual church-member who is interested in her art, not in religion. It may be that religion does not enter into her scheme as applicant for the position as soloist. She wants a little spending money and so she has in mind only a business arrangement. She may have no interest at all in Jesus Christ and His church.

What of the style of music? Anyone who has listened to the Hallelujah Chorus in Handel's Messiah—and who has not?—must be impressed with the inspirational qualities of dramatic music. It should be noted that the thrill comes not only from the music but from the emphatic distinctiveness of the words. There is no mistaking the reiterated

"Hallelujah" or the slow, sharp words of the triumphant phrase "And He shall reign." In instrumental music the mood is conveyed by the composition and its rendering, but in vocal selections the words have a purpose. Certainly this is so in religious music. How often in church are the words sung indistinctly? Where is the worship then? How often director, choir and congregation are satisfied and elated if the singers have "shown off!" Musical rather than religious effect is the primary aim. A quavering voice, off the key, that is the outpouring of a devout soul obviously has more value than an anthem faultlessly but thoughtlessly rendered if the teachings and spirit of the New Testament have any relevance to church music. The conclusion is not that poor music, ill-rendered is meritorious in itself, but that the primary function of church music is to lead the people into the presence of God and to inspire them in faith and service. Except for its religious theme, the standards of the concert hall are usually the standards of the church. Again it is worldliness.

It is sometimes asserted that the church has vested interests and therefore is impelled to accept without protest an economic order that is not Christian. A champion of the status quo for its own protection the church has hindered progress and turned from the common people. This aspect of worldliness must in all fairness be examined more closely. It is based in part upon the assumption that some other economic system—say socialism to displace capitalism—is more nearly Christian. The assumption is at least debatable. Those with keen sight for the maladjustments and inequities of our economic order often have a blind spot for the imperfections of a supplanting system. They identify Christianity with their own economic theory and utter diatribes in denunciation of the church. This is not just. The pulpit generally has not hesitated to criticize our economic delinquencies and church assemblies, sensitive to criticism of "reactionary" tendencies, have inveighed against injustices. In a measure, too, the church must conform to economic structure. It is the penalty of organization. Churches generally are corporate bodies created and recognized by state legislatures. They are naturally forced into the mould of our present order. Large sums of money are in the treasuries of churches and agencies of churches. The treasurer with a proper sense of responsibility does not keep funds in his bureau drawer, but deposits them in a bank. So he conforms to the prevailing economy. Within the church are economic conservatives from temperament or conviction as well as economic radicals whose radicalism stems from disposition or reason. The radicals will storm demanding immediate and drastic changes. They will become impatient of delays or disagreements. The conservatives are wary of fundamental changes that may bring disaster. They do not want the church to shoot off like a skyrocket—and descend like one. This condition of discussion is not an unhealthy one. The true criticism of the weakness of the church in allowing the world to superimpose its pattern upon the life of the church in its economy is that the church has accepted not only the standards, but adopted the practices of an economy that is too selfish and materialistic. This has already been noted, in part, in the statistical and organizational obsession of the church and its glorification of business methods imported into religious institutions. It has failed to perceive that the great need of America is not more business in churches, but more Christianity in business. But the prime example of the importation of the ideas of our economy into control in the churches is disclosed in their attitude toward its ministers.

The principle of a ministry in one form or another has been accepted by virtually all churches. With almost all the practice is to create a paid ministry. In accordance with the economic concepts that hold in this country the payment of salary confers power upon those who do the paying. The old saying is that he who pays the fiddler may call the tune. Many churches "hire" a minister. When that very objectionable word is discarded in favor perhaps of the better dressed term "engage" the belief that the minister is the paid servant of the church rather than the unpaid servant of God yet holds the helm. It might be said that the hand that controls the till also holds the tiller.

When a minister is invited to become pastor of a church, the invitation is piously termed a "call"—an implied recognition of the belief that God has something to do with it and that the minister was originally divinely called to the particular service designated by the name "ministry." But the meanings latent in the "call" are sometimes incongruous with the exalted language with which the invitation is extended.

First there is the most Christian consideration of age. The chairman of a pulpit committee called a denominational office on the telephone asking for the recommendation of a minister for the vacant pulpit of his church. In a breezy voice the chairman said, "We don't want anyone over thirty-five." There is nothing extraordinary about that although most churches have made the age limit ten years more. They don't want anyone over forty-five. That there is the least inconsistency between the sacred definition of the ministry as a life-calling and their stipulation of youth as the prerequisite for a pastoral position never even occurs to them. That God is confined to men under forty-five for his service is one of the unwritten but firm dogmas of the church in general. Why is there this insistence upon youth? One does not hear of a pulpit committee that says "Our first requirement is a man of prayer." Perhaps it may happily be taken for granted that ministers do pray. But other relevant questions are unasked or have a subordinate place. One might expect a committee to explain "Our church is at a great center where people naturally congregate. We need a minister who can present the gospel to this milling crowd" or "We have a school that requires the attention of one versed in education" or "We have people who need spiritual guidance, a friend and counsellor." Apparently no man more than forty-five is capable of a real ministry, at least not in a new position.

It is customary before calling a pastor to pray that the selection may be made under divine guidance. But when a prayer is actually though not audibly made, "O, God, give us the minister of Thy choosing (provided he is in his thirties)" it seems hypocritical twaddle to the unbelieving world as it sneers at the church. There is delusion somewhere. Even from a worldly viewpoint it would seem as if experience might have value, that an older man might by reason of his age have qualities which are deficient in youth; besides practice teaches an older man so that he can learn to do twice the work in half the time without expending as much energy as was required in the experimental period of youth. But the appalling inference is that experience does not count, that the ripeness of faith that only the years can bring, that the spiritual enrichment of life resulting from the accumulated treasures of Time are both subordinate to some magic supposedly resident in the young man. There is the confession that qualities of spirit are secondary to the physical freshness and vigor of youth. In this the church has gone beyond the world that ruthless as it is has glimmerings of hard sense in valuing experience. Of course it does not follow that a young minister is devoid of spiritual power or that years necessarily and mysteriously endow a man with it. But the blasphemy of an arbitrary age-limit is evident to the cynical world if not to the church that seems to think that if draperies are religious they are not diaphanous and perfectly conceal the dead bones of ecclesiasticism. Obviously there is room for the young man with his daring and new ideas. But even daring and new ideas are more a matter of temperament than of years. There should be places for both youth and age. Youth will not be excluded. Maturity should not be.

The minister is commonly called not only to a church, but from a church. That the enrichment of one church may mean the robbery of another does not enter into the scheme of things. It is usually a precise imitation of the business world where a man is enticed by the prospect of a better position. Just as in that business world there is a scale of salaries. One of the inducements to a minister from a church that wants him is a larger salary. It marks a promotion. The graduation of ministers and churches follows closely the way of industry. Consequently we have priced prophets. Inequalities of ability are indisputable. There are incompetent ministers as there are incompetent physicians and incompetent lawyers. There are men who mentally would not measure up to the responsibilities of some pulpits. Spiritual attainment is not a substitute for brains and brains are not a substitute for spiritual attainment. Only the mind suffused with the light of the Spirit of Christ is a Christian mind. The scholar is required for research in Hebrew or Greek. No amount of spiritual character can supplant a knowledge of languages for investigation in the areas of languages. Brains should be consecrated and consecration of brainlessness will not meet the demands of Christian scholarship. The problem set by material inequalities and differing financial compensations is a real one. It seems insoluble and the reason is that the church has institutionalism so imbedded in its structure that it is forced to find some working method that is far from ideal. But equating ability with financial compensation and the rating of ministers by financial standards is a strange interpretation of New Testament teachings. It is further illustrative of the infiltration of the standards of the market place into the sanctuary of God.

We should have to begin over again—as perhaps we ought—and refashion the church. Its adit into the social order of Main Street has imposed upon it the secularism that is characteristic of that thoroughfare of modernity.

A visitor from another planet would suppose that the finances of the church would be provided by the spontaneous gifts of a people who were so enthusiastic about the gospel of Jesus that they would continually give freely and generously of their substance for its support. Instead our visitor would be introduced to diverse not to say devious ways of raising money for the church organization. Commonly there are suppers—in competition with the restaurant across the street—bazaars—in competition with the department store on the corner—orders are sought for Christmas cards—in competition with the stationer a few doors away. These are the most common and perhaps the least harmful ways to keep the treasury filled. That gambling through games of chance has been practiced by churches is as true as it is disgraceful. Professional money-raisers are engaged. Campaigns are organized with teams that go out after a "pep" talk to stalk possible contributors and by the most effective selling methods which they have been taught in many a lesson on sales-talks beguile their victims into liberal giving. The church worker is instructed that he has something to sell and he must acquit himself as a good salesman of religion. So the church has borrowed the nomenclature of business. Its money-raising activities certainly smack of the practices of secular society.

In order to stimulate interest and giving it is a common practice to offer incentives such as inscribing the name of a church that has reached certain set goals on a roll of honor. Regularly churches receive denominational credit and public mention for achievements. Such favorable regard is not just a courteous and appreciative acknowledgment of work well done, but something to be striven for. It is not a serious defection, just childish perhaps, but an outsider acquainted with the profession of Christianity might wonder why worldly motives should displace or even supplement the dynamic of love for Christian service.

One would suppose that the world might be flattered by this imitation, but though the world may be irreligious it is not without acumen. Instead of commendation it has condemnation. Whatever justice there is in this judgment it should be tempered by the realization of a certain inevitableness about it. Churches are not in monastic separation from the community. They are partakers in its life. There would be no advantage in wearing one coat weekdays and donning another one for Sundays. To some extent, too, the church has moulded the community. It is not easy to draw lines of demarcation. A common practice of the world is not necessarily wrong. Jesus remarked that the children of this world are wiser than the children of light. We might learn of them. It is also true that ideas are so confused and purposes are so interwoven that understanding should precede judgment. And unredeemed human nature is tenacious in the best of men. No Utopia has been reached, but there are imperfect, struggling, failing men and women some of whom, at least, have caught a glimpse of the light and are sincerely trying to follow it. Yet, although excuses may alter our opinions of people, they never can alter facts. In the thought of fair-minded sceptics the church has taken on the hue of its environment perhaps as protective coloring against hardship and persecution but at a great cost through the loss of qualities important for spiritual dominance if not survival. After all charitable allowances are made, the American church is guilty of this sin of worldliness notwithstanding its constant protest against secularism.

The second count in the indictment of modern Protestantism in America is its lack of brotherliness. Such a lack is in fact a repudiation of Christianity. That which Jesus condemns, the church condones. There is no stain on the seamless robe of His teaching. There are no exceptions to His demand for righteousness. Whole goodness for the whole man constitutes His conception of life. But Jesus' understanding and mercy combined to set forth vividly His forgiveness of sin. He sensed the terrific power in the upsurge of human impulses. He walked into the midst of sinners not with the disdainful and censorious strut of the Pharisees, but with the compassionate step of a Savior. Repentant men and women conscious of their own weakness wanted His help. A woman of deservedly blemished reputation fell in tearful contrition at His feet. She heard no word of harsh rebuke, but tender words of forgiveness and encouragement. If there was gentle censure in the conversation of Jesus with the woman of easy habits at the Well of Sychar it opened her conscience and heart for the outpouring of courtesy such as she had never known. Jesus was accused of being friendly with taxgatherers and sinners—the spiritual and social pariahs of His day. There is a noticeable contrast in Jesus' attitude toward recognized sinners and toward those who were guilty of unbrotherliness. We can account for this only as we understand that unbrotherliness is a deliberate sin and one that denies the fundamental principle of Christianity which is love. Read His censures of the Pharisees for example.

It must not be forgotten that kindness and love are found within the church, but since the profession of the church is what it is that is expected and taken for granted. The conspicuous and too general prevalence of contradictory qualities is what tips the arrows of cynics with effective venom.

Disagreements, disputes and quarrels are so frequent in churches that it is only the occasional one that develops into a display of physical force or legal battle that is sufficiently news to warrant printing the story in the press. When some years ago an Irish Catholic policeman was summoned to avert disaster in the business meeting of a Protestant church and urged the members to act like Christians, the newspapers did not fail to acquaint the public with an account of the quarrel. Such a degree of belligerence as to require the interference of police is happily infrequent. The padlocking of the church door against a minister or a faction of the church or the refusal of one group in the church to allow an opposing group to use the building with the consequent division into the group that uses the church for so-called worship and the group that, denied the use of the church, assembles in a home for so-called worship is news that has appeared more than a few times. The number of churches that owe their establishment to a "split" is sad witness to the divisiveness and quarrelsomeness of church people. At one divided church meeting over which the author of this writing was induced to preside because he was an outsider and fair-minded, the two factions of nearly equal size were physically divided by the aisle from one another. Every one of the faction supporting the minister of the church sat on one side of the aisle. Every one of the faction opposing the minister sat on the other side. The physical division was clean cut. So was the mental division. The lamentable truth is that there are very few churches that go along for a period of many years without some conflict that causes the walls of what is called the temple of God to tremble from vibratory angry utterance, if it does not shake the very foundations. The explanations are various. Sometimes there are personal feuds. There are churches where some members will not speak to others. Sometimes matters of policy are involved. One church split because of a disagreement about changing location. The old building was worn out. So far there was agreement. The majority wished to build in a "better" neighborhood where there was the promise of a future for a Protestant church. A large minority maintained that the old neighborhood swarmed with people and should

81

not be deserted by the church. After acrimonious disputes, the majority built a church in the neighborhood they considered desirable. The others insisted upon remaining in the old location and displaced the old building with a modern structure. Disagreements about locations for a new building are not at all infrequent explanations of church quarrels. Very often the display of human nature not noticeably touched by grace is exhibited toward the minister of the church. Now the minister is human. The perfect one has not yet been found. Occasionally there is a minister who is labeled "quite impossible" and not without a large measure of justice. Sometimes a minister is arbitrary. Sometimes there is one with no tact. Sometimes there is one whose policies are ruinous or at least patently inadvisable. Extreme cases are generally understood and if the attitude of the church in opposition is at all Christian, there is little criticism. But when the attitude is not at all Christian and when the attack upon the minister seems to a large and reasonable number of people to be unjustifiable, there is the criticism that in itself is sufficient indication of the opinion of a great number of people who are not fundamentally irreligious that the church has little good to offer. A woman of considerable prominence in her community, the daughter of a minister who however was not living, and herself a nominal church-member remarked, "We need the churches. Support them. And keep away from them."

Instances of unworthy treatment of worthy men by the churches that they serve are so common that the community takes them for granted—not without a sneer. A few years ago there was in a certain church a man fairly well known in his denominational circles who made a practice of vilifying his pastor to everyone—even a perfect stranger casually met—who would listen to him. The minister was a man of good character, good spirit and good ability. The church, the larger part of which, could scarcely approve of such outrageous conduct did nothing. Probably it did not want to antagonize its prominent member. That he may have been insane at least upon the subject of his obsession did not excuse the church. At another church a member having lost the savings of the minister entrusted to him as friend and financial adviser turned upon him and announced that if the minister left he would give a sum of money to the church. Since this member was joined in his opposition by a considerable number of other members, the minister did leave. The record of the donation seems lacking. The minister concerned was a good and capable man. The trouble, of course, was bruited about the neighborhood. Another case involved a minister of outstanding ability, pre-eminent in many ways. His character was unimpeachable. A large number in the church turned on him with relentless opposition. Throughout the minister showed a spirit that was beautiful in its exemplification of Christian teaching. But the opposition increased to persecution. In another instance the financial leader of a church spent an afternoon ringing doorbells to stir up votes to accept the resignation of the pastor at the church meeting that evening. By a close vote the resignation was not accepted and the pastor continued but the breach continued also. Soon there was another split. The minister, rather ignorant but well-meaning, had shown poor judgment and lack of tact. That was the case against him. From time to time one hears of the contemptible suggestion of withholding subscriptions to force out a pastor unpopular with a faction. A friend remarked to the writer, "I had an uncle who was a minister. He became a bishop, but what abuse he had to take in one of his churches!" There is no need of multiplying illustrations. To contain all would require volumes of encyclopedic dimensions. The point is that these stories, although they do not make the headlines of the newspapers, are well known in the communities where the respective churches are located. The church is judged accordingly.

On the other side, it is true that ministers are often recipients of many kindnesses from the churches they serve. If intangibles were susceptible to measurement and it could be proved—as possibly it could—that the kind outweighs the unkind—it would be irrelevant. That this unkindness is not rare—rather general—is the point. That the churches fail in their primary profession blots out their worth to many observers. The causes vary but in general are obvious and therein lies the damage in public opinion. Basically the cause is human nature unreconstructed by grace. Some people in churches, as without, are born troublemakers. Some are just mean. Some are resentful because of real or fancied personal affronts. Some are angered because their theological or social prejudices have been offended. A restless few are always wanting a change. All offenders attempt rationalization. Seldom will one whose conduct has been inexcusable confess his wrong-doing even after time has elapsed to allow quick tempers to cool. The most contemptible words or actions are justified by some high-sounding sentiment. It is "righteous indignation," it is courageous combat against wrong ideas or measures, it is commendable opposition to a tyrant or an oligarchy that exercises too much power, it is faithfulness to noble convictions, it is a determination to protect the holy ark, it is for the good of the organization—alas! organizations forever displacing the kingdom of God! It is usually a minority—sometimes a minority of one that disgraces the church by its un-Christian spirit, but too often the majority adopts a policy of appeasement to avoid trouble. It fails in this because the news of acquiescence in manifest wrong reaches a disgusted public. To allow a few good people or a good minister to suffer so that disturbers of the peace may be mollified only adds one disgrace, which could be avoided, to another which could not for people who insist upon creating a disturbance cannot be deterred. If they have not the Christian spirit it cannot be created in them by legislation or decree. Meanness and trouble-making are not confined to the Christian church. But in business for example, such conduct will not be tolerated. A man will curb his inclinations toward evil for fear of losing his job. The church by reason of its democracy and tolerance offers a free platform to those who would be squelched on any other rostrum, when they attempted to vent their disagreeableness. Against the pure white profession of Christianity even grey looks black. People in general are aware that it is impossible to prevent the occasional emergence of an un-Christian spirit in a Christian community but they expect the church to proceed in respect of it on higher ground than a secular institution. It doesn't. They see little practical difference between a church and a fraternal order and sometimes the difference is in favor of the fraternal order. The spirit of love is the claim of the church to practical distinction. The church, in the judgment of many, has lost its distinctiveness. An impartial and considered opinion would be that there is more of the genuine Christian spirit in the church than anywhere else or than its hostile critics will admit, but it is in the individual and does not permeate the church.

The third count in the indictment of the church by its critics—including its best friends—is that it is indifferent. In apostolic times the simplicity, universality and beauty of a religion that was just what multitudes felt that they needed met with enthusiastic acceptance by an increasing number of converts. The historic events that contained the Christian message were recent. Jesus was almost contemporary. From the disillusionment and confusion of paganism the gospel burst like a new sun in a world of chaotic darkness. No wonder the converts to Christianity were enthusiastic. Nearly two thousand years have passed. The good news has become an old story. The familiar hymn even in its exultation over the perennial freshness of the gospel calls it the "old, old story." We have not been brought up in heathenism. From our earliest recollection, we have known the story of Jesus. We have been brought up on it. While spiritual light may still flood the soul with its glory and cause the heart to dance with joy, while the gladness of such an experience as the affirmation of allegiance to the Lord Christ may ring the chimes of ecstasy, for very many who are sincere in their declarations of faith, there is no quickening of the pulse at the rather natural consummation of the cumulative influences of teachings that began in earliest childhood. For many others who should be classed as thoughtless rather than insincere a profession of faith is conventional. It is the thing to do. There is a somewhat perfunctory expression of loyalty to Christ and a foggy-minded acquiescence in Christian teachings that have always seemed vague and remote. It is an expected consequence of this mixture in one body of the varying degrees of seriousness and comprehension with the loss of freshness in a narrative that is familiar that the enthusiasm attending a surprising and wonderful discovery should diminish. Furthermore, we are all creatures of moods. Unfluctuating interest would not only consume us, but would be dangerous as fanaticism starting a destructive conflagration. We are not here to start consuming fires, but to kindle steady lights. Even that is difficult for our moods tend to carry us below the normal. But allowing for fluctuations, lights may be relatively constant. There the church fails. If one believed what one who is a Christian is supposed to believe would he not venture all things, endure all things that the gospel might be known to all men and be applied to all conditions of life in all the world? In order to maintain the personnel at missionary stations and prevent the whole enterprise from slipping there is a succession of campaigns and "drives." If

86

these are successful it is because of intensive efforts of leaders to stimulate liberal and even sacrificial giving in those who are interested. Obviously "drives" should be unnecessary. There should be a constant flow of information and there is a place for exhortation lest men become "weary in well-doing." Nobody supposes that there is nothing to do except count and then distribute the greenbacks that in a steady stream deposit themselves upon a secretary's desk. But the pressure methods with their technique of salesmanship are necessary consequences of apathy. According to tables of comparison published from time to time the American people and apparently this includes a large number of church people, are more interested in motion-pictures, chewing gum, tobacco, than in the extension of the kingdom of God.

It is commonly said that an attendance of one third of the membership of any church on a given Sunday makes a good record. How many can be counted upon regularly because of their constant interest? How large a proportion of the members of any church cares enough to assume definite responsibility in the work of the church? And how often is interest in the church as an institution subordinated to interest in the religion for which the church is supposed to stand?

With all our progress in knowledge and our emphasis upon education members of the churches know less of the Bible than did their grandparents. College students coming from supposedly Christian homes are ludicrously ignorant of the book that holds the record of Christian revelation. The explanation of it all is indifference.

In all these conclusions we must preserve the distinction between "general" and "universal." The defects are general; by no means are they universal. Painful though it may be to contemplate these conditions we cannot resort to the soothing syrup of rationalization to obtain peace of mind. We cannot conjure up a moonlight of romanticism that will hide the rubbish in the vacant lot while it suffuses the distant hills of idealism with luminous beauty. The truth is that the church denounces secularism and is secular. It revels in studio paintings of a perfect society and goes out and plows crooked furrows, sowing with the good seed, dissension and malice. Discarding royal robes of Christian love it dons a business suit to ascend a throne of spiritual prerogatives. At least not only the cynical outside of the church and those others without who look with regretful detachment, but many humble, saintly souls within have come to the conclusion that the church is far from guiltless. There is this difference: the cynical sneer and exaggerate; the detached are sincere but myopic; the humble Christian is saddened by these defects but is also aware of the grandeur and achievements of the church. He refuses to allow failure to annul triumphs. He believes that the only hope of cure is through candid acknowledgement and diagnosis of the ailments.

Chapter IV

THE CHRISTIAN MINISTER

To put it bluntly a surprising number of people look upon Christian ministers as a little peculiar, not to say freakish. They think the ministry contains a larger proportion of the effeminate, eccentric or fanatical than do other professions or business. At the best there is a tendency to regard ministers as a class apart. Why in the world should a bright, capable young man enter the ministry?

Undoubtedly there are men in the ministry who would be more useful following the plow or handling saw and plane at a carpenter's bench. This might be said of the members of any profession. However state laws set up standards for the practice of law or medicine for example, while the requirements for ordination to the Christian ministry are purely ecclesiastical and vary. In some denominations the standards are almost entirely theological or emotional or a combination of the two. Men who have not gone through the eighth grade of an elementary school are ordained to the gospel ministry. If it is argued that there are exceptional cases—and every man considers his case exceptional—it is to be answered that a reasonable minimum of preparation is feasible for all and none will be injured by it. Furthermore there are in a few instances only, attainments that compensate for these educational lacks. Often the deficiencies in education are just to be added to other deficiencies of men whose only claim on ordination is their desire to be ordained. Character with sincerity of faith while indisputable prerequisites for ordination are not reasons for it. Not long ago a four year old boy regularly ordained created news when he performed a marriage ceremony. When such abysmal and amazing travesties on proprieties not to say religion are actual, is it astonishing that the ministerial calling is regarded with a quizzical look by many within and without the church?

Let it be observed at the outset that ministers are cut on the same human pattern as the rest of mankind. They have as many horns as countless others and no more wings than a multitude of the unordained. Yet it may be said that those in general who have been set apart to the Christian ministry are upright, sincere, earnest and idealistic, with a faith that demonstrates its reality in works.

The fine and manly qualities of many ministers can scarcely be questioned and refute the assumption that ministers in general are of a peculiar breed. Athletes including football players, baseball players, track men are not rarities in the ranks of the ministry. It contains some of the world's greatest scholars. It holds a large proportion of men of leadership and executive ability. Within its number there are men of courage—even the heroism that makes them martyrs. The history of missions contains chapter after chapter relating stories of men of magnificent mental and spiritual proportions. All are not of so large a calibre, but the majority are capable men who are neither effeminate nor freakish.

Consider the young man who decides upon the ministry as his career. What has determined his choice? The conventional and pious reply is that he has been called. In the larger sense and the one that has real significance, every man is called to become a follower of Jesus Christ and there can be no follower of our Lord who is not willing to serve Him and our fellows. The idea of ministry is not only implicit, but explicit in Christian discipleship. What, then, is meant by this particular call?

Naturally, the explanations will vary. Some will tell of a mystical experience, a voice that called as the voice of God is said to have called "Samuel" in the Old Testament story. Some will tell of a particular experience in a public meeting for self-dedication or a conversation that awakened a sense of responsibility for service or a verse of Scripture that seemed like an index finger singling out the reader for the work of the ministry. Some will say that they were restless, unsettled, and unhappy until they interpreted their continued mood as an indication of God's displeasure because they had not yielded to the opportunities for service offered in a minister's work. When they determined to turn to that vocation life changed, the tension relaxed, peace resulted. Some will relate the influence of a minister, a Sunday School teacher or a godly Father or Mother and will trace the decision to enter the ministry to such an influence. There are others who will affirm that as idealistic and Christian youths they desired that their lives should count for the promotion of good and helpfulness to people. They considered that their talents and bents particularly suited them for the ministry of the Gospel and concluded from sober reasoning that they could best fulfill their ambition for helpful living through the life of a minister. This they believe constitutes a call of God.

Nobody should depreciate the validity of experiences that are elusive because they are individualistic and unusual. As indicated above, a thoughtful judgment would maintain that all men are called to follow Jesus Christ and that calls included a responsibility for service. The particular form of service to which one is called depends upon the particular gifts of the individual. One man may be called to a ministry of a business man for a Christian business man should be, in the less technical sense, a minister of Jesus Christ both in his business relations and in conducting his business with the progress of the kingdom of God as basic motive.

91

Business is necessary to supply the needs of life. A farmer may raise his crops for the glory of God. In India Sam Higginbottom, a Christian missionary, established his school of agriculture in the belief that he could serve God by teaching the natives improved methods of farming that would save the lives of babies and of adults too. Was he less a Christian minister in following the example of his Master in caring for fundamental physical needs than in preaching the gospel to people handicapped not only spiritually but physically as well because of undernourishment? Medical missionaries some of whom no doubt would be failures as preachers have given sacrificial evidence of the service rendered by Christian physicians. There are Christian doctors of medicine of the same mould here in America. They are ministers as much as those who stand in pulpits. The lawyer who is more interested in promoting justice than in collecting fees may in and out of his profession be a Christian minister. The working man who does his part in creating goods and whose motive and influence are Christian is included in the Christian ministry. For the non-liturgical denominations the ordained minister differs from his fellow Christians only in function. In denominations that believe ordination confers power or authority not available to the unordained the situation is somewhat different, but there would be agreement with this broader interpretation of Christian ministry. But the ordained minister whether his "call" is the result of the unusual experience or of consecrated reasoning believes that he can best serve God by devoting all his time to the work of the church. That is the practical distinctiveness of his "call."

The young man who is set apart for the ministry does not exalt himself above others and he is not naive enough to suppose that he is entering a career where only spiritually super-men and women will be encountered as his parishioners. He does not expect the placidity of a lake so protected by surrounding mountains that nothing stronger than zephyrs will disturb its tranquility. He has some knowledge of human nature. Yet he is idealistic. He holds the Christian calling in high esteem. Some glint of eternal glory makes the church luminous to him. He rather supposes that reasonably good judgment, kindness, patience and faithfulness will quiet storms before they reach the velocity of a tempest. He has deliberately enlisted as a soldier of his Lord and does not expect to spend his days in the pleasant safety of a garrison far removed from the front where the battle rages. Rather like a good soldier, he is impatient to go to the front line where there are fighting and danger. He sees many forces in the world opposed to the kingdom of God —forces of greed, profligacy, hatred bringing devastation and misery and he is eager to combat them. He wants the redemptive power of the gospel to conquer souls, transform human relations and reclaim areas geographical, industrial, social, for his Master. The church he regards as an imperfect but devoted army for Christ.

In varying degrees there comes a process of disillusionment. There are ministers who would disclaim any great degree of disillusionment. There are others whose vision has been permanently distorted and whose ardor has been quenched because of the shock of it. Probably none is exempt from the experience. Too often the minister discovers that his energy and time must be devoted to meeting foes of one sort or another within the church. Instead of leading a company to the conquest of evils without, there is the unending necessity of rallying the indifferent within to such a support of the church as will enable it to combat with strength the hosts of unrighteousness. He discovers within the church all the kinds of evil that the church is set to oppose: cupidity, quarrelsomeness, hatred, intolerance, race prejudice, complacency, love of money, secularism, social snobbery, militarism, the full catalogue of sins. Further-

93

more he will learn that the church will impose upon him its own standards. It may attempt to take the bloom from his idealism. In a previous chapter we have seen the defects of the church. These will compel him to accept as his main task the building of the organization even at the sacrifice of the principles that he has been taught are the fundamentals of Christianity. He will be judged by his record and that means largely a statistical record. He must increase the membership of his church. If the means of doing this are not quite ethical, few will scrutinize the report provided the results are pleasing. He must take the responsibility of raising money and here, too, the methods need not be too spiritual. In short, he must make and keep his church "a going concern." If he does not succeed in this his days there are numbered and the number is not of the higher mathematical variety. If at any time he desires another pastorate his success in obtaining it will largely depend upon this kind of a record. He may be a man of splendid character, a good preacher, a friendly, helpful pastor and possess other talents but if his record does not show unquestionable organizational success regardless of circumstances he is at a decided disadvantage. Thus he is driven to excesses of zeal. A minister in one city wrote to the pastor of a church in another city to obtain a letter of transfer of a member who had moved to the town from which the minister wrote. The next mail brought a letter of protest from the member to her pastor. She had suspected a request would be made for her letter without her permission. She did not wish to transfer her membership for several reasons. That sort of thing happens too often to be treated as a rare occurrence. A minister of known liberal beliefs invited to his church an evangelistic team that was almost uncouth and that represented the very ideas and methods that the minister opposed. Why did he invite them? Because he must have baptisms for Easter Sunday. Apparently he was on shaky ground with his church.

He knew he was expected to have converts for Easter. In the desperation of necessity he turned to what seemed the most likely means of obtaining them. Without Easter baptisms his tenure would be limited. At least he seemed to think so.

There should not be too harsh a judgment on these zealous men who in pursuit of definite, concrete objectives have lost some of their principles on the way. They are not always consciously wrongdoers. In the intensity of purpose with the accompanying demands of strenuous activity they have had no time to weigh such moral niceties as are involved in their methods or if they have found moments for reflection they—like most of the rest of humanity—have rationalized their procedures so that they are in good conscience. Certainly, too, there is a host of ministers who will not be deflected from their idealism by any temptation to gain success through the sacrifice of their most exacting scruples. But there are times when it takes courage to withstand the pressure to obtain some temporary success at a price to conscience. These ministers will often be supported by men and women in the churches who deplore with them the worldly standards to which the church has yielded, sometimes unaware of what it was really doing. Compelled to accept practices that are inconsistent with their conceptions of absolute right must they reject the church altogether? That, they believe, would be a greater wrong. Forced to choose between evils, we do not at all surrender our perception of the absolute good or of our allegiance to it. Caught in the wheels of worldly ecclesiastical organization the minister going along with that which is not consistent with what ought to be, may ease his mind by public announcement of the ideal and exhortation to approximate it. But he realizes he is powerless to make the church over. He is not a dictator. Besides, as we know, complete renovation is difficult if not impossible. What is the ideal in all its perfections? How should we go about attaining it? How indeed can we right the wrongs that are obvious and of least difficulty to correct? Anyone who will sit down and consider the complexities of the situation will understand the state of mind and of heart of the finest spirits in the Christian ministry. If the pastor of a church desires to be called to another church he will discover that he is involuntarily in unavoidable competition with fellow-ministers. This accepted fact may be glossed over with unctuous words, but nobody is really deceived. Pastoral changes are often, perhaps usually, the effect of influence as much as preferment in politics is fostered by it. The winner is backed by someone within or without the local congregation who has influence. His own merits may be studied. Doubtless they will be. But his name will be tossed aside unless it has an introduction that will make an impression. What can the individual do about it? The facts are not changed because in theory pastors are appointed by a bishop or some other authority outside of the local church. Influence counts. Rivalry and competition are not banished there.

In view of all circumstances it is a matter for comment but not for wonder that the minister perceives that he is more than he expected a member of a profession with all its dignities, honors and appurtenances and that he is less than he might wish the follower of a calling. The two are not mutually exclusive although the idea of the profession tends to displace the idea of the calling. Etymologically the two words are much the same in meaning. Practically we detect a difference as the words have developed. The profession emphasizes the human, the calling emphasizes the divine. By profession we ordinarily imply work that is mental rather than manual, that presupposes technical preparation setting the possessor apart in that respect from those who have not acquired it and that is usually a means of remuneration. A calling may be simple, humble, and technical preparation may or may not be essential. Above all, it suggests conviction and response to something above the self. The professional is set apart more by external distinctions in recognition of his attainments or functions. The one who is called may not at all be separated factitiously from his fellows. Any distinction comes from the perception of inward qualities and their application in situations that may be quite informal.

Thus there is presented a question that perplexes. It is assumed for cogent reasons that a minister should have educational preparation for his work. A thoughtful and educated man recently asked "If a man believes the gospel and such teachings as those of the Sermon on the Mount why should he not go out and preach these simple things without first spending years in school?" Of course, the answer is that he can. There is no reason that he shouldn't. But to preach the gospel is not the same as to become the minister of a church. The complex duties of the pastorate require preparation. It is not just a matter of preaching the gospel. It includes that. Even in this if a man is ordained to a career as a minister he may be expected to have some grasp of the subject he is talking about. A preacher who speaks with evangelistic fervor and makes no pretense to scholarship will through the sanction of ordination with the examination it entails, be expected to have some knowledge of his Bible and not to flounder about in a swamp of ignorant and incoherent emotionalism. If as custom dictates a man is to stand in a pulpit Sunday after Sunday, expound the Bible and apply the unchanging principles of that book to the changing problems of the day, he must be versed in the Bible and be prepared also to understand and interpret the eternal truths in which he believes. The many diverse tasks that demand the attention of the church today require thorough preparation upon the part of its clerical leaders. All men have neither equal abilities nor identical gifts. But men who are capable must be trained to meet the intellectual questions of the day with answers that will command respect. Educated people in the pews cannot be expected to find direction for their thought or help in solving their personal problems or in gaining a spiritual point of view in respect of world conditions from a man in the pulpit whose ignorance is as indisputable as is his sincerity. The minister as a leader in civic life and in religious education must be equipped for his work. All this seems obvious enough. But a tiny question wriggles through these disquisitions on the necessity of an educated ministry. It is this: Does not this education tend to alienate the minister from his people? In large numbers they are not educated. Jesus with His unique personality mingled in a natural way with the common people. A minister today may count among his most loyal friends uneducated men and women with spiritual intuitions and attainments beyond his own. But if we speak generally what must honestly be said? The pastor without any thought of condescension may minister to the humblest of his parishioners. He may give himself to them with utter unselfishness. But the fact remains that there are limitations. The educated man seeks companionship among the educated. He may have an interest in Plato but he cannot discuss literature with the semi-literate. He may be a student of history or physics, but he cannot have intellectual companionship with those who know nothing about Waterloo and whose notion of physics is the primitive one of a series of direct divine interventions in the earthly sphere, nor can he discuss the complexities of religious questions that dog his own thinking with men who cannot grasp them. The query persists: Are not ministers educated away from their people? In particular instances—and these not few —the answer is partially but emphatically negative. Ministers of acknowledged scholarship have so abounded in affection and sympathetic understanding that they have been beloved by the common people. Missionaries with fine intellectual training have gone out to live with degraded people sharing to an admirable and amazing degree the lives of the poor, ignorant, diseased and filthy people to whose betterment physically, mentally, morally, spiritually, they have magnificently devoted their lives. They have become friends of the outcastes. Yet in missionary lands most missionaries today do not live in the mud hut or on the scanty diet of the people whom they would help. If they tried they would not survive and their ambition to help would not be realized. Love will break through mental inequalities. Yet the answer is only partial. The emotional sects that spring up with almost seasonal regularity are evidences of the distance between the average church and the more emotional less literate of the masses. These people, whatever the intelligence quotient of most of them might register, need religion, want religion and many of them are capable of religious responses that are genuine and will germinate in a religious living comparable to the living of their neighbors in the churches of higher educational attainments. It is true that these new denominations indulge in deplorable extravagances, often make a virtue of ignorance, debase and discredit religion by their antics, crudeness and irrationalities, but they gain converts that the more dignified churches have not been able to interest. Clearly the trained minister belongs to a profession. That makes men look up to him, treat him with respect, but it does not make them feel that he is one of themselves. We cannot substitute ignorance for knowledge, or abolish education for ministers. Nor can we neglect the common people. There is no perfect solution to our problem. A minister may not allow his consciousness of professional status to crowd out his sense of vocation. He may cultivate a humble spirit. He may develop understanding of the outlook and requirements of the masses and pour out his affection upon them. In that way he may overcome the handicap of his professional standing. It should be added, however, that thoughtful Christians whose souls are troubled will look to the pulpit not only for intelligent interpretation of life's problems but also for intellectual stimulus and ability to cope with attacks upon Christianity from educators who in these days from the chairs of traditionally Christian colleges sneer at religion and impress upon their students the claims of a naturalistic philosophy to their allegiance. The admirable tradition of the pulpit as expositor of a religion that commends itself to men's minds as well as their hearts must be maintained. But probably in the very congregation that demands intellectual pabulum of the preacher there will be those who are not interested in that sort of sermon and are unable to appreciate it even though the speaker rejects technical terms in favor of a simple vocabulary. These people require spiritual food. They must have it. Gifted preachers may be able to give to the intellectual group on one Sunday and on the next deliver a sermon that is simple and practical and therefore of benefit to the entire congregation. But the division is not obliterated. The less gifted preacher will sacrifice one or the other of his group of listeners. The saying that a preacher should spread food on the ground where both the giraffes and the donkeys may reach it is not quite fair to the giraffes who are built to reach up. Thoughtful people demand thoughtful sermons. Others want entertainment only. There may be incidental religious benefits. A large auditorium in a California city was filled week after week for what purported to be a religious service. It really was a vaudeville show in six or eight acts. The programme changed weekly. A short religious talk by an attractive looking woman was included and all the acts were allegedly religious, but it was as truly a show as any on the boards of a theater in the city. But it was what people wanted.

It should be made plain that education and intelligence

are not equivalent. There may be intelligence without formal education and there may be formal education without too much intelligence. And the basis of Christian fellowship is spiritual rather than intellectual. With these qualifications and surveying the large number of people whose intellectual interests are on the level of the motion picture theater and the average program on the radio, it must be admitted that education indispensable for the ministerial vocation accentuates its professionalism. This is but one of the dilemmas with which the minister is confronted.

The young man ordained to the ministry will be compelled to give some thought to his economic status. It will be an embarrassing thought. Anyone who expects to get rich through serving churches as pastor must have checked his common sense in the ante-room of his first church. It is not true as is sometimes asserted that every man who enters the ministry makes a financial sacrifice. The alternative for some ordained men would be a very subordinate position in business or in agriculture where the stipend would be less than he receives as a minister. The average minister, however, has to plan carefully to make ends meet. Notwithstanding all this, economic motives are not eliminated at the ordination service. The minister usually hopes for financial advancement in much the same way that the young man who enters a business hopes for a series of promotions that will be marked by increases in salary. Promotion and economic considerations tend to become standards of success with the minister. If he is called from one church to another he wants the change to bring a higher salary. Not seldom the amount of salary becomes a matter of negotiation. The man called requests more than the church at first is ready to offer. It is a case of pious bargaining. There is a practical ministerial hierarchy in denominations that scorn all that bears the name of hierarchy. The man with the largest church and the highest salary gains the recognition that such a position entails. There are high salaries paid to ministers. One minister recently remarked to another, "I know six vacant churches that pay $10,000," with an intimation of the desirability of these positions. There are numbers of city churches where the pastor receives a larger salary than the majority of the members of his church. To affirm that salary is not a consideration in changing from one position to another—perhaps *the* consideration—is just contrary to fact. This is recognized—taken for granted. Over and over again one may hear a statement made to the chairman of a pulpit committee concerning some man under consideration for the pastorate of the church. "If you want him you will have to offer him more money," or "He is out of your class," meaning beyond their financial ability to reach his demands, or "You can't touch him. Do you know how much he gets now? A thousand dollars more than you expect to pay." Again you may hear the chairman of a pulpit committee remark, "You can't expect to get a first class man for what we can afford to pay." Churches are graded largely, not absolutely, by the amount they pay. Ministers are graded largely, not absolutely, by the amount of financial return they can command for their services. These classifications are so taken as a matter of course that few give even a passing thought to their justification. The distance between the little country church that pays its minister little more than $1,000 and that of the great city church that offers a salary of $15,000 is tremendous even after a liberal allowance is made for the difference in cost of living in a rural area and that in a big town. The minister of a prominent church was offered an increase of salary and declined it. The newspapers regarded it as news and gave considerable space to relating the story. The minister in question was a man of fine, unselfish Christian spirit who would never be accused of putting financial returns first. But after all his salary was $10,000. That his refusal to accept more should be classed as news worth printing in a metropolitan newspaper is a revelation of the commonly accepted ecclesiastical economic standards. For a minister to decline an increase in salary is really not so uncommon as all that. But it remains true that ministers in general are swept into the professional estimate of their calling. They want to get ahead. They want professional success.

Before we administer blame we must consider extenuating circumstances. First a minister becomes a part of a system as we have said that he cannot overthrow or even correct. Then he is compelled to think of his family. There are men who would suffer poverty without complaint themselves, but they are unwilling to ask their families to live on a lower scale than others with whom they associate. A minister properly desires to give his wife and children reasonable opportunity for decent living. He believes that they should have sufficient nourishing food. He wants his wife to appear well clothed. He rebels at the idea of having his children marked off from others in the school because of shabby clothes. He feels a responsibility for giving them educations. For these purposes he needs money. The Roman Catholics have solved the problem by insisting upon a celibate clergy. If a Catholic priest wishes to sacrifice worldly possessions he may do so without bringing poverty upon others. But in this economic solution the Catholic church has done that which is repugnant to Protestant churches. It has set its priests off as separate from the laity. The priests suffer under the disadvantage of having no home life and cannot enter into the lives of their people through the common joys, sorrow, decisions of rearing a family. Protestants believe that the minister should live a normal life. For most men that is the life of the family. The affection for his home and his sense of responsibility for wife and children, admitted virtues, compel the minister to have this interest in their economic conditions. He may not be mercenary, but the salary he is to receive will not be a matter of indifference to him.

The minister is expected by his church to dress well. The cost of the clothes of the average pastor of a church would contrast with the prices paid by Kagawa for his notoriously inexpensive clothes, but, then, Kagawa's (even in summer) would contrast with Gandhi's. In the pulpit the minister who does not wear a gown—and gowns are not cheap—is expected to wear garb that befits his professional standing. His pulpit clothes will probably be more expensive than the ordinary suit that will likely be the best attire of many of his congregation. In every day life the church will feel that it is a reflection upon itself if the minister is not as well dressed as most men of other professions or of business. There is an appearance that is regarded as proper that must be kept up. His telephone is really a necessity for his work—but he has a telephone. In these days he cannot do justice to his work without an automobile. He will be criticized if he does not have one—but he has a car.

It is not fair to infer that the minister is a luxury-loving person who lives on the fat of the land. A large proportion of the ministers have a hard time to make ends meet and keep up the appearance demanded of them by their churches. And earnest ministers are not unfamiliar with sacrifice. They will go without things they not only want but need in order that they may give to some worthy cause in which they are interested. To be sure, they are not alone in this. Earnest Christians who are not set apart by ordination will deprive themselves of luxuries or of what might be called necessities in order to help others. Some save even in their poverty that they may be able to give to those who are poorer than themselves. The conclusion is that the ministers of America are a conscientious, generous group who for the reasons stated may not neglect their economic situation.

Perhaps the most amazing evidence of professionalism

—and also the most shocking evidence of perversion of the simple idea of a divine vocation—is that of sermonic contests. One of the most reputable and indeed finest and worthiest of Christian weekly newspapers sponsored such a contest. A selected group of ministers was invited to submit sermons to be passed upon by competent and disinterested judges. The winning sermons would be published. Indeed it is not an uncommon practice to offer prizes for the best sermons submitted in some competition. Imagine the Apostles Peter and Paul entering a sermon contest! It would certainly take a large dose of an imagination-inducing drug to produce a picture of that. Shocking indeed—but no astonishment— no disapproval expressed anywhere!

Why, then, should we persist in a professional ministry? Why should not other churches imitate the Society of Friends, commonly called Quakers, in their earlier practice of not having a paid ministry? The Quakers really supplied the reason for a regular ministry. They were—and are— notable for their good works, especially in their habitual service to the destitute and oppressed throughout the world. Regardless of race, creed or location, if there is need the Quakers can be counted upon to be there with their disinterested but loving help. Impressive as these services were the Quakers limited their ministry in other respects by their refusal to adapt themselves to a changed world. They are not conspicuously evangelistic. Their meeting-houses did not attract the public generally as the other churches do. They were aggressive only in their quiet works of charity. But the modern world needs the right kind of aggressiveness. By right kind is meant an aggressiveness that is not flamboyant or aggrandizing but is motivated by Christian love. In this sense the apostles were aggressive even to turning the world upside down according to their foes. Paul was aggressive in traveling from country to country, from city to city, preaching and teaching everywhere. The Quakers apparently have sensed this for the modern Quaker service is much like the service in other churches. Happily, there are occasions when the old idea is revived.

There is practical value in a beautiful church building located where it will attract attention. The distinctiveness of architecture of a church is itself an advertisement for religion. In days past the steeple of the church rose high above other buildings in a community. Today the modern skyscraper outtops the church. Once upon a time Trinity Church in New York City thrust its spire above the neighboring buildings. Long since there has been a change. Skyscrapers cluster on that lower end of Manhattan Island that furnish the famed sky line of that city. Trinity has become a pigmy in the land of the giants. Yet it is by no means lost. There it stands at the head of Wall Street, the financial center of America. The banker or the broker coming from his office looks up the street and sees the fine old church. It does not pronounce its benediction upon all the transactions of "the Street," but it may give pause to those who are bent on reckless speculation or immersed in materialism. It surely does symbolize the relation that ought to exist between finance and the kingdom of God. The beauty of the church and the gospel it presents shine out upon stock exchange and banking-house. Wall Street and America would suffer an irreparable loss were Trinity Church removed from its historic corner.

Far uptown in the same city the lovely edifice of Riverside Church stands just off the Hudson river. Its towers can be seen from far up the river. The church is located in the intellectual center of the city. Right beside it are the buildings of Union Theological Seminary and close by is the campus of Columbia University. The temple of religion rears its head among the halls of learning. Truth of the spirit appropriately accompanies the education of the mind.

There is a psychological gain in the presence of a lovely Christian church on Morningside Heights.

The ordinary residential neighborhoods contain churches that lend a sanctity to the homes about them. In the slums where poverty and filth breed crime or at best produce a bare, dull, life the church is the witness of a better life where kindness and helpfulness prevail. The mere building may be a bright spot in shadowed lives. The very edifices themselves require organization. Their spiritual upkeep no less than their physical cannot be haphazard. The signs on nearly all churches contain not only the name of the church, but also the name and address of the minister. If the church is to mean anything to its neighborhood there must be someone easily found and accessible to render service to all who need it. In thus designating a minister the stranger understands at once that the church has made someone available upon whom any may call without fear of intruding—someone who is set apart for the specific purpose of giving spiritual help to all comers. It is helpful in a little village to have a minister who is not compelled by business to give only the fag ends of his time to spiritual ministries of the sort mentioned. It is quite conceivable that a shopkeeper is a man of deep faith and wide sympathies who could give help to those who waited upon him with more wisdom and practical benefit than the ordained minister. But the shopkeeper must take care of his customers. His days are taken up earning a living. Being the kind of man he is he will find time to help his neighbors, but the minister although he is beset by many duties will surely count caring for the spiritual needs of those about him as his first duty. In the cities with the relative impersonality that they create it is as imperative that someone should be designated for spiritual ministry as that physicians shall have their names and profession posted conspicuously enough to be seen by those

107

who require physical attention for reasons of health. And if a church is to relate itself to the daily needs of the neighborhood it will be necessary to have a programme extending beyond Sunday services. Since most people are engaged during the week in earning their livings someone must be paid while he devotes his full time to the activities of the church. In these days of a complex society and the resultant specialists the man who can give all his time to church work is a practical necessity. Much idealism must be sacrificed to that thing: "practical necessity."

It is neither irrelevant nor a digression to have thus considered at some length the justification of the position and function of a modern church in a community for that explanation also justifies the profession—not the professionalism—of the ministry.

As we have already hinted, the minister who is placed in a busy parish will find himself in the midst of a bewildering whirl. Even a brief experience will initiate him into the realization not only that there are numerous demands made upon him, but that the nature of the ministry itself is compounded of many exacting and widely differing departments of service, each requiring its own kind of skill.

First of all the accepted prerequisite for everyone is the cultivation of his devotional life. He who would help others must himself receive power. The path to the perpetual springs of divine grace must be kept open. The minister must not yield to the temptation of neglecting this even though a multitude of duties intrudes. There is no argument about this. It is not just a prelude to the performance of his duties, but is a strain running through all that he does.

Of the many functions of a minister preaching stands foremost in the public mind. Preaching, however, even by itself involves much else besides the mechanical preparation and delivery of sermons. The minister is expected to preach at least once—in many churches twice—of a Sunday. How many outside of the ministry have given thought to what it means to prepare one or two sermons week in and week out, year in and year out? There are preachers who are unequal to the strain. At the end of two or three years they are homiletically exhausted. Therefore they do not remain in one church for more than that period of time. With some old material and a new start they can continue with a degree of effectiveness in another pulpit. A wise minister remembers that his audience must listen to him every Sunday. It is the same preacher and largely the same audience. Even with the best of preachers to listen to, the congregation may find it a little monotonous. It is only fair to his hearers that their minister shall make every effort to keep his sermons fresh and interesting. To accomplish this he must study and read. The Bible makes the first claim upon his attention. After all we are people of a book. Whatever changes have occurred to cause many to accept so-called modern views of the Bible and no longer regard it as a kind of stenographic record dictated by God, the fact remains that we belong to the Book and the Book belongs to us. Its pages are the greatest source of inspiration to even the most "modern" of ministers. Christian people have ever come to the Bible for food and never have they gone away empty. They want the Bible. They ought to have it. The preacher will read it reverently and studiously. He must become steeped in that Book. If his interpretations of the Bible are to be valid he must consult the commentators from whose scholarship alone he may get the sense of those passages that require for their understanding a precise knowledge of the text and of its backgrounds. Furthermore, the preacher must read books. They will be books of all sorts. They may include history, philosophy, psychology, science, sociology, literature both prose and poetry. He must know what the world is thinking about. He must keep abreast of the main contributions of modern knowledge. He must read the newspapers and the magazines not for recreation, but to inform himself of current events. His hearers will come to church from their newspapers. They want him to throw light upon the events of the day—not with the expert knowledge of the reporter or the historian, but they want to know where God enters in. They want the principles of religion applied to modern life. They would relate current history to the kingdom of God and the Christian life. They expect the minister to be the interpreter. Even more they want comfort and counsel for their own daily lives. They have trials, temptations, decisions to be made. They look to their minister for help in meeting these problems that may be as old and unchanging as humanity such as the grief brought through death or as new as modern science, such as their children's addiction to radio programmes and television the benefit of which the parents question. And if the minister is to meet his people on their own ground he must know what they are reading. To know that he must have some acquaintance with modern fiction. Besides all this, in the conditions we have described in discussing the profession of the ministry, the sermons are to be delivered at stated times. At eleven o'clock or whatever the hour may be the minister must enter his pulpit prepared to preach. Like everybody else he has moods. Some days he will be eager to deliver a message that has thrilled him in its preparation. But he must wait until Sunday. Then if his enthusiasm has not cooled at all he will pour out his soul to his congregation. On the other hand there may be Sundays when he compels himself to enter the pulpit. He is not in the mood for preaching. Perhaps his mind is sluggish and he feels that the message he has prepared does not do justice to the great message of his Master that he seeks to proclaim. Nevertheless he must keep to the schedule. Yet ministers will consider preaching a privilege and a responsibility. It makes demands upon them. In addition to regular pulpit appointments the minister will be called on for funerals, for addresses of one sort or another throughout the week. This combination would appear to require the full time of a man. Preparation of sermons and addresses may be in a variety of ways. A few will fill their minds through voracious reading and rely upon skill, experience and readiness of speech for actual composition or delivery. Most will give a fair proportion of time to the form a discourse will take. But woe to the man who relies solely upon quick wit and fluency of speech! Some years ago in one of our cities there was a preacher who did that. He rather boasted that he prepared his sermons on Sunday morning after he had reached his church. He was a glib speaker and was confident in his ability to weave something sermonic from a few tawdry threads. His success was short lived. It could not be other. The late Doctor S. Parkes Cadman was known at times to pick up an outline on his way to the pulpit and then preach an excellent sermon. But Doctor Cadman was omnivorous in his reading. His was a constant preparation. His mind was an overflowing granary. Whatever the method employed preparation of sermons consumes hours each week. But this is just the beginning of a minister's work.

In large churches there is likely to be a division of labor because there may be an assistant or even a staff. But the minister in charge is ordinarily held responsible. Sometimes assistants, especially women, are employed almost wholly in clerical work leaving the rest of the work to the minister. Division of labor may be forced because the burden of work is both physically and mentally impossible for one to carry. In general, and this applies to many large churches, paid assistance, if there is any, is limited to clerical service. With allowances for individual cases as indicated the minister must be an educator. In the larger sense this is universally true for the pulpit has an educational function. More particularly the minister is the responsible head of an organization that includes a school where the children of the congregation and children of the neighborhood receive religious instruction. This is one of the supreme opportunities of the church: to influence boys and girls in the Christian way. The immediate task in the school will be relegated to a principal or superintendent, departmental leaders and teachers. Not all of these will possess either natural gifts or technical training—far less that wonderful combination of the two—to prove competent educators. It is the minister who must supply training classes, encourage educational ideals, try to construct standards for the church school. Working with the material he can get, his task is more difficult than it would be if he could shift the training of the children to those who could carry on independently. This is the beginning but not the end of his tasks as an educator. He will probably want to conduct a communicants' class for boys and girls who seem ready to enter into definite church membership. Then if he regards seriously the needs of his parishioners he will institute and probably teach classes in adult Christian education. Bible study, missions, social problems will occur to all as appropriate and important subjects for adult education in the church. In our daily school system in America a superintendent of education or a school principal fairly exudes busyness and exhales a sense of the importance of his work. But he is backed by the authority of the State. His teachers have received technical training. His schools are carefully graded. Tests and examinations determine the promotion of his pupils. Teachers are held accountable for results. Pupils who fail or make no effort to learn may be detained after school for discipline or individual instruction. There will be special schools or classes for those who are slow or mentally below the average. There will be recognized methods for dealing with the slow of thought. Compare this with the educational efforts of the church. Education is voluntary. Children may be kept out of school every time the parents decide to drive into the country to spend Sunday at Grandma's or visit a friend. Absences require no excuse. Enter a strenuous objection and the child will be taken from that school and sent to another where there is enough worldly wisdom to refrain from any objection to repeated absences. Whether or not lessons are prepared will depend upon the interest at home. Almost invariably precedence will be given to the requirements of the weekday school.

Finally the educational task is made still more difficult by the absence of adequate gradation. Our modern church schools are graded, to be sure. There are departments that range from the nursery to the adult division. Within the departments classes are graded and lessons are graded to the classes. There are promotions from department to department all with appropriate and impressive ceremony. But the gradations are determined by age not by achievement. A bright boy with a high intelligence quotient is in the class with a dull one with whom learning is a slow, halting and perhaps an almost impossible process. When promotion time comes the whole class will go on regardless of ability or achievement. How often would anyone dare to leave a pupil back? He may not be ready for promotion, but the boy must not be hurt and his parents must not be offended. Sometimes as much damage may be done to the development of a child by hurting him as by promoting him undeservedly, but the practice of indiscriminate advancement puts a brake on education and creates a situation of great difficulty for the teacher. With no enforceable standards education approaches the farcical. The situation is similar in adult classes. There the teacher is beset with the dilemma of teaching those who have the ability and willingness to learn at the expense of those who cannot or will not think, have almost no backgrounds of knowledge, but wish a kind of sentimental tickling of their emotions or on the other

113

hand of pleasing the dull and uninterested who as adults have considerable to say about the desirability of retaining minister or teacher and, consequently, of sending alert minds and eager lives home empty.

Yet the minister is keenly aware of the terrific, pressing and recurring crises in the world which the child soon must face. The minister knows that the attitude of the boy or girl in this world will be largely determined by his religious and moral training. The minister reads the reports of juvenile delinquency and is aware that judges and educational leaders both believe that the most hopeful remedy is in religious training. For better or for worse the public schools do not teach religion. In any event it is the office of the church primarily to give religious instruction. No conscientious minister will minimize the importance of Christian education. He has available all the help that his denominational experts can provide. The actual application of the principles, however, belongs to the local church. There are failures in our public schools notwithstanding the authority of the State back of them, the technical training of professional teachers within them. What, then, can the church school with its handicaps and limitations be expected to accomplish? There is no touchbutton system that will illuminate lives. It is all personal work. The minister who does not take his duty as an educator seriously is deficient in one of the essentials of his work.

The pastor of a church is expected to be a financier. A Board of Trustees has legal supervision of the finances, but even when a capable Board assumes responsibilities for income and expenditures, the minister will be called into consultation from time to time. There are few who can act like a notable preacher of a few years ago. When summoned by his trustees to a meeting he went, but upon learning that the concern of the meeting was with ordinary financial arrangements, said, "Excuse me, gentlemen, if that is all you want of me, I'll go for I have an interesting book to read." Perhaps he could afford to be independent, but he ought not to have been. The minister knows better than anyone else of projects, some of them of his own planning, that require financial expenditures. He must advise about the relative importance of projects. And if the church because of a depression or for any other reason is in financial straits, it is almost always the minister who must assume responsibility. It is usually he who must make appeals for money. The success or failure will depend usually upon his ability to create a sufficiently strong sentiment to avert the threatened deficit and disaster.

Along with this the minister of a church has the duties of an executive and administrator. A busy church is divided and sub-divided into a variety of organizations. Not only is there a Board of Trustees, but there is usually a Board of Deacons or Elders, there are women's societies, missionary organizations, youth fellowships, boy and girl scout troops, weekday religious schools, a number of committees. Depending upon the location and particular interests of the church there will be other organizations. A church, for instance, that specializes in neighborhood service for the under-privileged of the community will develop agencies for this work. The church school is not only an educational institution, but a somewhat complicated organization. And every church will have some publicity work. There are calendars to be prepared, letters composed and sent to the membership, items of news for the daily papers. Even a relatively small church will have a complex organization. The responsible head is the minister. Where there is a church large enough to have a staff of paid assistants and secretaries there can be a sharing of responsibilities. Generally speaking it is the minister in charge who must correlate and supervise the organizations within the organization that there may be a minimum of friction and duplication with a maximum of coherence and unity both in spirit and in the practical attainment of the purpose of the church. In a large church with a correspondingly large programme the executive and administrative office will be a busy place and require quite as much skill and work as a moderately sized business. In a small church the work will be exacting in a different way. The minister will have few capable leaders upon whom he can depend. Consequently he must attend to details himself and learn how to accomplish some things with an insufficient supply of helpers and it may be with few of them competent. The anomaly of the minister's position in respect of executive and administrative functions is that his workers are his bosses. He is held responsible, but his powers of direction are limited. In business an employee does what he is told or his place is vacant. In a church where service is voluntary, plans are carried out or not carried out according to the decisions and whims of the workers. If they are dissatisfied they may stir up trouble and dismiss the responsible head. He never gives orders. He makes requests. If they are not complied with he is powerless. There certainly is no reason why arbitrary authority should reside in the hands of a minister. He must consult with his advisers and be guided by their judgment. A headstrong minister with poor judgment and equally poor ability to plan could easily ruin a church. But to the degree that his power is limited, his responsibility should be limited. It is not so. All his plans may be rejected with resultant failure, but the responsibility for the failure remains upon him. What minister has not had the experience of appointing someone head of an important committee only to be chagrined by the discovery that the one appointed was doing nothing at all in the assigned work, but blandly pursuing the accustomed way oblivious of all responsibility? It is true all was explained in the beginning and there was an expressed willingness to accept the assignment. What can be done? A little prodding?

Oh, so gently! If he just looks and then turns over to go to sleep again, what is the distracted minister's recourse? Remove him and appoint another in his place? That drastic remedy had better remain untried for there will be offense. No one seems to be offended more quickly than one who without excuse refuses—if one can characterize permanent dilatoriness by so decided a word—to do the job he has promised to do. Unless there is some tactful fashion of inducing him to resign, he must be permitted to retain the post and block the way of someone else who might be appointed in his place. Meanwhile the work to be done is left undone. One of the marvels of the church is that a minister hampered as he usually is, can achieve administrative success. It would patently be impossible if there were not able and consecrated men and women of the congregation who will get into harness and pull without thought of recompense, indeed forgetful of themselves.

Not by any means the least important duty of the minister of a church is that of the pastor. Broadly speaking the service of a pastor comprehends four common, human needs. First there is grief. Old as the world death comes with a kind of shock of newness. No one ever seems ready to part with those who are loved. As a general proposition, everyone knows the inevitability of this experience, but in its concrete realization none is prepared for it. In the hour when affliction has stunned a soul with his bludgeon there is a call for someone to revive the stricken through the stimulation of faith. It is natural to expect the minister to bring comfort. Indeed it is an opportunity to be coveted—that of ministering to those who sorrow. To lift the curtain even a little so as to disclose the calm of abiding realities is a task that brings its own compensation. But it is nervously exhausting for the minister. Secondly there is illness. People who are ill want encouragement, cheer, peace, faith. It often happens that a spell of illness acts as a check rein on one who has

117

gone at a thoughtlessly selfish gait. One who apparently has not entertained a serious idea for years suddenly is faced with the issues of life. He is not only susceptible to spiritual guidance but craves it. He wants someone with a pastor's heart. Even a brief illness, not severe, usually creates a desire for some spiritual ministry. Physicians have been known to say to ministers "You can do more for the patient than I can." Here, then, is service for a pastor. Thirdly, there are problems. Problems are of all kinds. There are those caused by loss of money, or employment when one does not know where to turn. There are choices that must be made; there are decisions that cannot be avoided. There is anxiety about the son or daughter. There are questions about church relationships. There are matters of faith and understanding about which help is needed. There are concerns about spiritual living. Here there is scope, for the sympathetic ministry of a pastor. Fourthly there is discipline. This perhaps is least considered as a pastoral office. Yet it may be that nothing is more nearly related to a pastoral gift. It is the most difficult of all. A minister will hesitate to say a disciplinary word. If he is conscientious he will be afraid of assuming a Pharisaical role. Who is he to admonish another? Has he not his own sins to confess and to overcome? His may be of a different sort from those of a parishioner whom he would help, but they are just as truly sins. Is it not at least an impertinence for him to appear as a spiritual superior? He thinks he might easily be asked "Who are you to rebuke me?" And sure enough who is he? In these days, too, we have a wholesome fear of intrusion. What is the right of a minister to admonish another in what may be regarded as a personal matter? He must not pry into the affairs of others. It is, thus, peculiarly difficult to do pastoral service that involves in any measure the spiritual discipline of another. The situation is changed when one voluntarily makes his minister a confessor. Here he is put in the position of confidant and helper. A woman says "I'm terribly tempted. What shall I do?" A young man inquires "I've broken all the commandments, is there any hope for me?" A minister is often the sole recipient of a confession of wrong, it may even be of crime. Everybody knows that confession is often times beneficial. The Roman Catholic church is a master of practical psychology. One of the most distinctive evidences of this mastery is the establishment of the confessional. Protestantism with its totally different belief about the authority of a church cannot institute compulsory confession, but a minister will realize that people must have a way for voluntary confession of sins. In this sense Protestantism has opened the way for this spiritual catharsis. To hear a confession, to deal not only sympathetically but with healing power with the confessor is a ministry of first importance.

There is considerable advocacy of the advantage of psychiatry to the pastor of souls. It is advice both good and dangerous. It is good because we know enough of the mental and spiritual organization of men to show us how interwoven are processes of the spirit. We know something accurate about mental ailments. There are definite diagnoses and there are techniques of treatment. Clumsy dealing with mental ailments may be disastrous. We cannot revert to old, simple dogmatisms of theology. While it is everlastingly true as so noted an authority as Jung alleges that there are peculiar powers of recuperation for the sick mind in religion and we of the church do not at all relinquish our faith in the restoring powers of divine grace, there are mental conditions that cannot be adjusted by the ordinary methods of religion. Christianity does not renew a leg that has been cut off. We don't expect it to nor do we disparage our religion when we say so. In order that the immense healing powers resident in religion may be used they must be channeled through acknowledged psychological media. A minis-

119

ter who through complete ignorance of the principles of mental therapy gives bad advice may seriously injure the one he would help. Therefore he should know psychiatry to some degree. The advice to a minister to study psychiatry has a dangerous side. There is always danger in a little knowledge. It is too breezily assumed that any intelligent minister may put a little time on the study of psychiatry and become a competent adviser of the mentally ill. It is not realized that proficiency in psychiatry requires knowledge, experience and aptitude. Knowledge and experience may be acquired, but aptitude is innate. To master to any extent the precepts of psychiatry it is requisite that there shall be more than superficial reading of books upon it. Initial ability is more than that. You cannot make a good teacher by the simple device of sending the aspirant for the profession to a school of pedagogy. He must have prior aptitudes for teaching. A school of art will not perfunctorily turn out artists or a course in poetry create poets. There is what might be called a kind of intuition and a certain sort of personality required to make a psychiatrist. Few professions require this native ability more than that of a psychiatrist. The advice, then, to the minister about studying pastoral psychology should be qualified. He ought to become sufficiently familiar with psychological facts and procedures to learn his limitations. Thus he will be cautious, apply the simple techniques of psychology to find out whether a particular case is for him or should be referred to a mental doctor. Whatever psychology he may learn will be helpful provided it does not give him overconfidence through supposing himself to be an expert. Some ministers who possess this aptitude may be effective amateurs and be more helpful than those professionals whom no amount of training will make thoroughly capable because they lack the prerequisite aptitudes. Within a narrower but still a vast area, every minister may exercise whatever acumen is his as a pastor. Most cases require sympathetic understanding and common sense advice.

Such is the Christian ministry of today. Can so many and so diverse abilities be united in anywhere nearly equal proportion in mortal man? The obvious answer is in the negative. A man may have one conspicuous ability—with the equally conspicuous absence of other abilities. He may be a great preacher, but no educator or an administrator or pastor and have not the least semblance to a financier. Another may be a wonderful pastor, but a poor preacher and indeed not proficient in any of the other requirements of a minister. There will be some with one outstanding ability and other gifts—perhaps not all—in a smaller proportion. Probably none will be equally good in all though some may have moderate abilities in several or all of the functions they are expected to discharge.

The apostle Paul knew better when he differentiated among gifts. They were gifts not qualities acquired through preparation at a school. Some have gifts as apostles, some as evangelists, some as teachers, some as pastors. But not all evangelists are pastors or all pastors evangelists. A minister was summoned by a woman he had known for many years for consultation about a problem. She said to him in explanation "I can't ask my own minister. He is a good man and is doing a good work, but he is not the kind of man you can talk to about this matter concerning which I need counsel." What did she mean? She meant that her minister lacked the gift of a pastor. The apostle Paul understood that kind of thing very well; the modern church understands it imperfectly. There is the expectation that all these qualities associated with the idea of a minister may be done up in one human package ready for delivery to any who wants it. The exigencies of our modern ecclesiastical organizations

121

make these impossible demands. It is reason for astonishment that the minister meets the demands of the day as well as he does.

We began this chapter with a description of the young minister whom the roseate finger of the future beckoned on. With the passing of the years the gesture of the future may have become a warning or even menacing finger. As we have seen it was not that the young man was so utterly foolish as to suppose that the way ahead was all sunshine and never rough. But the sanguine spirit of youth minimizes the effects of dark days and dangerous paths. The young man thinks he will not be deterred. He believes that somehow he will come through all right. Probably he will if he has faith, grit and determination.

It is essential to our understanding both of the ministry and the minister that we take account of this experience which may well be pivotal and consider it more definitely. To some there will suddenly come a sense of frustration. High hopes will crash. Or it may come as a gradual realization. He may feel that the wings of buoyant expectations have been clipped. Humdrum days, disappointments not on the low and selfish level, but on the higher plane of the spirit will bring a series of jars to any normal person. However this unwelcome awakening comes it is imperative that the minister shall find mental, emotional, spiritual equilibrium. He must learn that life may become richer, faith more certain even though there is an inevitable sobriety induced by events that turn back hopes and blot out plans. If the minister is to continue in effective influence and service two opposite results must be avoided. He must be aware lest disillusionment shall drive him into the gloomy valley of cynicism where because shadows are deceptive all things will be suspect. Others differently affected as they are subconsciously frightened or consciously shaken by disappointing revelations of life in realms called religious for which they were not prepared will grope for an escape from unwelcome realities and in the name of faith refuse to accept them. In thus escaping the valley of cynicism they enter the mythical paradise of illusion. In this safe retreat they either avoid all logical inferences from the undeniable presence of that which displeases them or see it under the more attractive though false color supplied by cherished, artificial concepts that interpret all their experiences. The result is that they are of no help in solving problems and their optimism is so superficial that it makes them shallow. It is from unsuspected, lonely crises that the worthy minister learns to endure.

Possibly the minister needs a mirror in which he may see his vocational self. Assuredly the churchman of the pew and the man of the world need a window in the wall of prejudice, criticism, misunderstanding, conventional judgment or sentiment or idealization that often separates them from the minister in order that they may see more clearly his points of view and the duties inherent in his calling. Failures, even collapses of faith should not be judged too harshly. The minister, on the other hand, who is clearly a man of God and walks with undaunted faith, unquenched zeal and benign demeanor bearing on his heart the cares of his people and serving them with sacrificial devotion has attained only through spiritual crises, agony of soul even though he has had invincible faith.

Chapter V

THE CHURCH AT WORSHIP

We hear much about worship these days. What do we mean when we talk of worship, especially social worship? We are not seeking a dictionary definition. What is the practical reason that impels a devout Christian to go to church to worship? Is it not a feeling of the need of God in his life? Of course God is not limited to a definite place or his appearance dependent upon a specific time schedule. God should be in the daily life and should dominate its issues. Prayer does not wait upon appointed occasions. Religious experience may have a measure of constancy. Why then should there be a church for worship? Is it not because of a sense of need for deliberate and exclusive concentration upon God? Each day is crowded with duties. All should be related to religion, but they are not religious in themselves. The irreligious may work in office or in shop beside the Christians and perform much the same task. The first is not consciously serving the kingdom of God. For the Christian doing the daily task in a Christian spirit and trying to relate it to Christian ends is not the equivalent of turning the mind exclusively toward God. And worship may be solitary. It may appropriately be in the church because the church is associated with that idea. It may conceivably be in the home or in the fields or in the woods. But because we are social creatures, no man living alone, there is a place for social worship. As social beings we are different from what we are as isolated individuals. There should be solitary devotional periods, but they are not a substitute for social worship in

124

the sanctuary. So a Christian goes in company with his fellows to make a direct contact with God. It is a place and time for expression, also for reception.

There are, however, wide divergences in the conception of what constitutes worship. We have a long stretch from the practices of the high church party of the Episcopal church to the simplicity of the old-time Quakers in their meetings. The Episcopal church in this country retains the official name of Protestant Episcopal although those who call themselves Anglo-Catholic disdainfully spurn the designation of Protestant. They are in the anomalous situation of being repudiated in the validity of their ministry by the Roman Catholic church while they disliking the Protestant label maintain against Rome the genuineness of their claims to apostolic legitimacy. Their idea of worship might be styled by the unsympathetic as an imitation of that held by Rome. If they would resent that at least it would be admitted that there is much in common between the two churches.

The Episcopal church as a whole is one in which forms are prescribed and dominant. The more evangelical low or broad church Episcopalian would allow some latitude in worship and would deprecate the primacy of ritual. An Episcopal rector of prominence has been heard to exclaim, "I am no ritualist!" His interest in the ritual might be explained on practical grounds rather than by high church theories. The use of liturgical service in the Episcopal Church is easily understood. In the Episcopal church you may expect the processional of choir and minister with the cross borne before. The service itself will consist of hymns sung by the congregation, probably an anthem by the choir, scriptures of the Old and New Testament read by the minister, prayers read from the Book of Common Prayer by the minister with responses by the congregation along with a confession of sins read by all. The service for the day will be prepared by the church in its manual and will be appropriate to the Christian calendar. There will, of course, be a sermon. The service will conclude with a recessional. (Why, a non-Episcopalian may wonder, do Episcopal ministers of all ministers inject into the beautiful and coherent service a series of notices about the work of the parish—something that is extraneous, interrupts the continuity of the service and might well be entrusted exclusively to the church calendar.) The manner of conducting the service will vary somewhat in accordance with the proclivities of the minister for or against the ritualistic. Some will bow before the cross, others will genuflect before it. This brief summary will serve to indicate that the worship in Episcopal churches is formal and prescribed. The service is in beautiful English and is marked by reverence and dignity. The prayers are comprehensive in their thought, based on an appreciation of unchanging human aspirations and needs. The modern worshiper, especially a cultivated person, will join in the service with a sense of the fitness both of language and thought for the expression of his own feelings and ideas.

The Episcopal church may serve as the best example of formal worship. There are other ritualistic churches notably the Lutheran church. The Lutheran church is thoroughly Protestant in its position. In the days of Martin Luther there was a clean break with Rome. There were not the gradualness and the vacillations of the Church of England in a transitional period. But Luther had no impulse to discard ritual. His attitude toward the Catholic doctrine of transubstantiation is typical. He could not accept it neither could he entirely reject it. So he compromised by means of his idea of consubstantiation. The Lutherans have retained the formality of their service and with it have retained the element of ritualistic beauty that inheres in most liturgical services.

126

The obvious defect of a set order of worship is that spontaneity is squeezed out. There is the ever-pressing danger that what was originally a medium for the expression of a vital experience will become stereotyped. Forms easily become formalities. One says the familiar words while the mind wanders over all creation. Verbal conformity creates a deluding judgment of duty performed. This danger is not by any means one to which everybody succumbs. On the contrary there will be those who affirm that the familiar usage over the years brings cumulative riches to the life.

Some of the non-conformist churches have undergone a metamorphosis in relatively recent years. Some have not. Not too many years ago the worship in the average non-conformist church excluded neither spontaneity nor crudeness. A ministerial gown or a vested choir quite shocked the congregation. The minister wore a frock coat and the members of the choir sported a full garden variety of flowers in their hats. The service was simple. The pulpit prayers were altogether extemporaneous. This particular kind of service has not only survived but has degenerated. There were many reasons for this acceleration toward the indefensible. First there are no restraints. It is inevitable that men with no taste or appreciation of fitness shall express themselves accordingly. And there is always the temptation to cater to the uncultivated. Thus the writer heard a minister pray: "O Lord may we not be like goats eating the circus posters from the billboards, but as sheep in thy green pastures." Especially does it hold true that in music descent is conspicuous. Years ago when Dwight L. Moody was moving two continents with his evangel, he was accompanied by his singer Sankey whose songs were almost as effective as Mr. Moody's preaching. The words were not notable as poetry nor did the music conform to the highest standards. But the words were simple and were not offensive to an educated ear for they often had the beauty that goes with simplicity and sincerity. The music had melody and was catchy. Revivalistic music did not originate with Moody and Sankey. It was heard in the spirited singing at camp meetings in the west long before. But the Moody hymns were printed in book form and obtained wide popularity. After the time of Moody and Sankey there were imitators. The merit of the gospel hymns of these evangelists disappeared. The words of the newer hymns often had little sense and by no stretch of the word could they be included in poetry. Many were silly jingles. The tunes fit the words. Their chief quality was that of catchiness. They were not suited either to arouse or express religious emotion. They were sensuous, not to say sensual. They induced excitement and motion. It was a travesty on worship.

There are churches that have been swept along by the current of crudeness. Dignity and reverence have no place in them. Indeed such qualities are despised as stiff and stuffy products of snobbishness. The purpose of these churches is to reach down to the lowest taste and not seek to lift taste to higher standards. There are those who seem incapable of improvement and it may be argued that we must accommodate ourselves to their kind of religious observance. There are those who could be improved in their tastes, but who are immovably set against improvement. They dislike the self-discipline of education. They are not only contented with things as they are, but they prefer that to which they are accustomed. If then, we peek in on many Protestant churches ostensibly at worship we shall see a gyrating minister on the platform—probably the pulpit has been removed as an obstacle to his ecclesiastical acrobatics— who shouts in many instances, in more or less ungrammatical English, shibboleths that are emotionally charged to stir the feelings of his auditors. The musical instrument will bellow forth in fast time the kind of sound that leads to stamping the feet or clapping the hands. There may also be an exhortation to that spurious fellowship engendered by "shaking hands with the one next to you." It is all crude enough and repellent to many people, but it would not be safe to affirm that there were no values for any. If a critical judgment might be ventured it would be that simplicity is not to be equated with crudeness and that there are greater possibilities in many people for development in appreciation of the better things than is generally supposed. This does not solve the problem previously mentioned created by the gap between the bright and the dull, the restrained and the highly emotional. It does suggest that experiments in the elemental ranges may avoid the extreme crudities that not only cater to deficiencies but worsen them. The Salvation Army long ago hit upon the device of putting religious words to popular tunes. It took the airs the common people were humming and made them the vehicle of religion, thus getting down to the people and making contact with them. The Salvation Army was designed to do a sort of work that the churches were not then doing too well. It was trying to reach the men and women whom nobody else reached religiously. The religious meetings conducted by it cannot be described as appealing to people of cultivated taste. Nobody makes that supposition. But the officers of the Army have had some training in practical psychology. Though their methods may seem crude to the casual observer, they are often very astute. Furthermore the Army sets its converts at work in a practical fashion for which they are fitted so that any emotionalism awakened by their unconventional methods of holding religious meetings finds an outlet in practical Christian helpfulness.

The change that has been noted in the more cultivated evangelical churches is most interesting. Forty or fifty years ago worship was unemphasized and undeveloped. Preaching was paramount. If the churchgoer arrived in time for the

129

sermon he scarcely considered himself late. Both in tradition and in principle the sermon is important in churches of this class. They are prophetic rather than priestly. If the sermon stimulates religious feeling and induces a religious response it is really a part of worship. Separation of the preaching from the rest of the service is unreal. This principle applies both ways. The period that precedes the sermon is not merely preliminary. It requires attention concerning its reason for existence. Churches began to give more thought to this. Why should they sing hymns? What hymns should they sing? What should be the nature of the prayers? It was not enough to answer that prayer is a necessary part of religion. Should not particular consideration be given to the pulpit prayers? What part should the congregation have in the service? In the old time the congregation usually had no vocal part except in singing the hymns. Those who asked these questions concluded that the service of worship in the average Protestant church was rather forlorn. There seems to have been a consensus of judgment that the services should be enriched. The easiest way to achieve this effect was to learn from the ritualistic churches; to borrow from them making what adaptations appeared appropriate. In the nature of the case there was no uniform approach or application. Only generalities can be used in describing the changes. Some features approached the universal. Choirs donned robes. Ministers began to wear gowns. Responsive readings were introduced. The congregation attained a larger share in the audible worship. Beyond this the variations were numerous. Processionals and recessionals of the choir were common. Confessions of sin were printed on the calendars in some churches and were read in unison by the congregation. Often there were moments for meditation. Prayers might be concluded with choral responses. Chants were not unusual. Pulpit prayers were given more attention by many ministers. They might be prepared and written

130

beforehand. There was more probability that when the prayers were extemporaneous thought had been previously given to them. Historic or otherwise appropriate prayers of the church or prayers composed independently by individuals were read without apology or hesitation.

Today the orders of service as printed on the calendars of various churches of much the same class will show considerable divergencies. The likeness will be in the substitution of a service that is more liturgical for the rather informal service of an older day. It is left largely to the local church —which usually means its minister—to determine the precise content and arrangement of the order of service. There is an advantage in this independence of prescribed forms and an accompanying danger. Freedom is always dangerous. There are always those who can be counted upon to abuse it. Where one is hedged about with restrictions it is obvious he will not run wild unless he jumps over the barriers and repudiates both authority and fellowship. In the free churches there may be that which will jar the nerves and be insufferable to sensitive souls. This is true not only in those churches previously discussed that specialize in jazz and other disagreeable noises, but in churches that try to incorporate the worthful into their services yet do not quite know how. They compromise in their singing by mingling the fine church hymns with the musical parodies on religion associated with the crudest and most extravagant sort of revivalistic campaign. And the anthems of the choir may scarcely be rated as music suitable for worship. The minister, too, may mar an acceptable service by interjecting comments peculiarly inappropriate. He may believe in extemporaneous prayer without having mastered the requirement of pulpit praying. His prayer may be so carelessly composed as to distract attention from its intent by reason of mixed metaphors, ungrammatical speech and ranting tones. His prayer may be akin to the newspaper in that it apparently aims to make the Lord acquainted with the events of the week. It may take the form of a second and subordinate sermon ostensibly addressed to God, but actually directed at the congregation. If spontaneity is to be retained such are the risks that must be taken. And it should be remembered that there are churches using free and independent forms that are excellent both in content and in manner of expression. There are pulpit prayers where spontaneity is not ruled out by prescribed forms that lift the worshipper to the sanctuary on high and conduct him into the holy of holies where he sees God face to face.

Of all the changes that have characterized the modern free church in forming its somewhat amorphous order of worship the most extraordinary has been the displacement of the pulpit by the communion table surmounted by a cross. This is sheer imitation, the reason for which it is difficult to discover. Possibly it arises from a dim or distinct perception that the cross is the symbol of Christianity and therefore should have the position of significance. But there is nothing incongruous between the traditionally central location of the pulpit and the symbol of the cross. The cross may—and often is—on a communion table that is directly before the pulpit. The vision of the worshipper sees the communion table with its cross and is lifted to the pulpit that does not at all obliterate the cross. Rather the one leads the eye and the mind to the other as they are both in the direct line of vision.

The peculiarity is in the implication of the altar as substitute for the pulpit. This modernistic arrangement sets the pulpit on one side with a lectern in a corresponding position on the other side. The altar is appropriately of primary significance in the Roman Catholic church because in that church worship is centered in the mass. The bread and the wine are believed to be actually transformed by the priest into the body and blood of the Lord Jesus. So in a

132

literal sense He is there as the sacrifice renewed day by day through the power conferred upon the priest. Protestantism holds a totally different belief. In fact the controversy over the Catholic theory of transubstantiation has been one of the most uncompromising of all questions in dispute. Even if the communion table as the emblem of fellowship were accorded first place in Protestant worship—as it is not—one would be put to it to bring out a sufficient reason for this change in so-called non-liturgical churches. The evidence that it is not accorded first place is seen in the fact that whereas mass is said every Sunday in Roman Catholic churches an observance of communion is usually only monthly, bi-monthly or even quarterly in most Protestant churches. Historically the Bible supplanted the altar in the Protestant conception. Views of the Bible have changed with a host of Christians as we know. But because it is no longer considered verbally inspired by very many it has not therefore been relegated to secondary rank for it contains the only early story of Jesus that we have. All subsequent lives of Jesus have been developed from the New Testament as chief source-book. It contains the narrative of the crucifixion. Without it we should have no gospel except what might survive in uncertain tradition upon the authenticity of which no check was possible. Because the gospel story was committed to writing at a very early date and found final and creditable authentic form in general in the four gospel narratives we have an historic ground for the Christian faith. The symbol of the cross is lifted from the New Testament. The pulpit that formerly and without question was the center of vision in the free churches invariably displayed a Bible. All that the cross symbolizes is likewise and primarily symbolized in that Bible. The worshipper looking up at the pulpit sees it not as a reminder of ungoverned and perhaps presumptuous oratory but as a proclamation of the prophetic spirit of the truths related in the Book. Sheer logic would continue to place the pulpit in the familiar position. The removal of the pulpit and its Bible both typical of the Reformation spirit and conception is bewildering. Apparently the best explanation is in the fact already suggested that when there was a realization of the crudeness of the forms in the average evangelical church the natural tendency was to look to those churches that had developed forms of beauty and to use them as patterns. A recognition of the precedence of the cross did not delve into the reasons for its priority in liturgical worship, but accepted it as it was displayed in churches that customarily used it as the principal representation of their conception of worship. There have been compromises. The idea of the altar has not vanquished the prophetic emphasis in favor of the priestly. With the new sense of the proprieties of worship the suggestion of an altar has not definitely indicated the reason for the innovation. This is quite in contrast to the distinct teachings of Roman Catholics. It may be remarked, too, that in these days when brevity in church services is the popular demand Episcopal churches hold to a short sermon while the free churches abbreviate the period of worship. This increased attention to ritual even to the imitation of the chancel is an interesting phenomenon that invites study, but it has not greatly affected the old ways in practice. From a pulpit removed from its former commanding position there may be prophetic fulminations and quite as much emphasis upon the function of preaching as in a church constructed in the older fashion.

We recur to our initial definition of worship: seeking contact with God for the replenishing of spiritual strength and the expression of religious feelings. The question is, "How should this be accomplished?" That will first depend upon the conception of God that we hold. The primary element in the Christian idea of God is that He is a Father. This idea underlies and embraces the principles of our

Christian faith. We talk much of the brotherhood of man as a Christian ideal. In whatever sense this may exist it is founded upon the prior idea of the fatherhood of God. Thus specifically in the Christian fellowship admittedly the idea of brotherhood is predominant and the designation is in common use however many and serious may be the lapses in practice. In the church even more emphatically than elsewhere there is predicated the fatherhood of God. The theologians with all the thrusts and parries of their interminable combats never contend about that. Today when the banners of Christianity are emblazoned with the captions of its social significance the fatherhood of God is insistently urged as imperative reason for the practical applications of these principles.

Just here there is a strange inconsistency between our fundamental Christian conception and our practice in worship. If in our thinking we regard God as Father, in our worship we approach Him as a king. And this is not the day of kings. We have drained out most of the Old Testament idea of God as king. We say it arose in a time when men habitually looked upon the community as headed by a monarch. Hence the head of the religious community was thought to be king. In our democratic time the voice of the people proclaims the ruler. This is applied to God. The only way He can rule in reality is not through the despotism of eternal creative power, but by the acclamation of His people. They give Him their hearts. They follow His ways much as children who love their parents will accept their superior wisdom and ever strive to please them because of affection. This is not to discard all divine sovereignty. But whatever sovereignty is predicated to God is sovereignty over creation, not tyranny over His children. No; there emphatically it is the guidance of a Father, not the edicts of a sovereign. Assuredly in worship we are not seeking a relation to majesty on high, but to a loving Father. We do not desire the exercise of sovereign power on our behalf, but the supply of grace from One whose capacity for loving His children is unlimited. Such grace is imparted through the touch of the divine life upon the human. Our approach in worship is to a God who "so loved the world." We may believe in Jehovah who sits upon the throne of the universe, but our imaginations stagger at the implications. We would draw away and not draw near. Whatever acceptance our wills may give to this king of unutterable majesty is the result of our confidence in a Father. We sing, "O worship the king all glorious above," but that is an expression of awe. We don't go to church to tremble at His might, but to wait upon His mercy. We are not courtiers doing obeisance to a king, but children obedient to a Father's love. The heathen may placate a creator, the Christian pleases a Savior.

Bearing in mind this distinctiveness of Christian worship with its emphasis upon communion with a God revealed supremely in Jesus Christ who invited men to come to His friendship with the utmost informality of approach, we may analyze the attitudes and acts that together comprise a Sunday morning's worship in church.

Everywhere hymns are sung. God has put music and poetry into our hearts. Thus singing is most natural. A daughter will sit down at the piano and sing a song expressive of her love for her father or mother. When she has finished she will turn around and smile and say, "That is for you." The parent will be touched at this sweet expression of affection and the room will be redolent of the beauty of the relation between parent and child. A young man sent his mother on her birthday anniversary a copy of Van Dyke's poems marking the poem the author wrote in honor of Mothers and of affection for them. It was a natural tribute. Similarly it is not forced or artificial when hymns are sung in church provided some thought is given to the appropriateness of the words as well as the tune and the genuineness of the sentiment reflected. It is customary to read the Scriptures as a part of worship. This has the same appropriateness as reading a letter or some other writing from a father to his children. The Bible is properly called the Word of God. To call it so does not imply adherence to any doctrine of verbal inspiration. In it we hear the voice of God in human speech that we can clearly understand. In all churches prayer is made. That plainly is talking to the Father. And that is natural enough. If it is objected that pulpit prayers tend to be formal if not stilted and in that lack the easiness of communication between parent and child, the reply should be made that when one represents a group speech becomes more formal. If, in a family, one child is selected to present some request of all the children, the representative of the family will not speak in quite the same way as he would if his approach to his father were purely individualistic. There is the same kind of difference between public prayer that includes the group in its scope and individual prayer. If the service in the church gives any place for silent prayer or if the public prayer is applied to himself and echoed by the worshiper that inaudible prayer will be more informal. So if the prayer from the pulpit is a cry for mercy, a conscience-stricken worshiper may well whisper, "Yes, Father, that means me." The confession of sin in worship is also part of the parent-child relationship. Every proper child who has done wrong will go to his parents and confess the wrong seeking the forgiveness that restores to the full the relation of confidence. An offering of our substance to the extension of God's work is a necessary accompaniment of loyalty and love.

Further consideration should convince us that the tone of our service is not really in agreement with the attitude toward God that we seek for ourselves and strive to instill

137

into others. Whoever heard of children approaching their father wearing uniforms and with the stately steps of a processional? In the courts of kings there is prescribed etiquette. A master of ceremonies may inspect all who present themselves to make sure that they have conformed to the requirements of court dress. They will be instructed about the proper manner of approach to the regal presence. Chants and responses carefully inserted at the appropriate places are quite in harmony with a presentation before royalty, but somewhat out of place in an approach to a father. The robes of the choir may be defended certainly as in keeping with the kind of service the church promotes and thus an improvement over the alternative of a choir in ordinary garb where there may be a riot of conflicting colors. That distracts from worship. Of course the real question is one about the necessity of a choir in the house of a father. The defense of the choir is on practical grounds and is inherent in our conception of worship as a formal service. It is purposely spectacular and generally sensuous in its appeal. The effect of all this is to force the idea "Father" into the background. Certainly it may be maintained that a church where you must face the right way at the right time, bow or genuflect at the right word has obviously adopted the etiquette of the court. It may be beautiful and impressive, but it implies the approach to a king. It does indeed save from the very objectionable procedure that makes for a familiarity that is really disrespect.

The Friends or Quakers in their worship historically represented an entirely different idea and one that receives scant attention these days. The underlying logic of their approach is quite simple and is not without convincing reason. Our Christian assumption is that God is everywhere. His immanence eludes definition: far more does it elude imagination. Somehow, mysteriously to be sure, God indwells the life of every believer.

> "And every virtue we possess
> And every victory won
> And every thought of holiness
> Are His alone."

Tennyson has said "Closer is He than breathing, nearer than hands and feet." Whittier wrote:

> "We need not climb the heavenly steeps
> To bring the Lord Christ down."

These poets in worshipful spirit only affirm a faith that we take for granted. When we sing the hymns we express our own acceptance of their faith. In addition, as has been emphasized, the Christian postulate is that God is our Father. We simply couple these ideas and conclude that our "Father, God," is present with us. If then we wish to make conscious touch with Him we naturally turn our minds to Him. By excluding thoughts that may be extraneous we find our Father, we may talk with Him, sing if we like, listen in the quietness to Him as a presence within. A simple illustration is that of a dear friend in the room with us. We are conscious of his presence in a way—perhaps we should say subconscious—but we are engaged in some task. It may be a task that is distinctly for the friend or at least meets his approval. But the task requires our direct attention. We are at a book or writing or making something or performing a household duty. After a while the particular task is completed at least for the time and we leave it turning our attention to the friend. Or we may sit in that sweet silence of tranquility arising from the conscious presence of the friend and an invisible and inaudible fellowship that it induces. There is, as most people know, this peace and joy from sitting in the room with one in whom we have complete confidence. Presently we begin to talk. Our fellowship is actively communicative. So, the Quaker may argue, it is with God. We are engaged in the work that life imposes on us. We must give it our attention. We should be far from leaving God out of it. We may seek to honor and serve Him in all things. But there comes the time when by ourselves or with other friends of ours and of God's we may devote our attention directly to Him for the expression of our affection and loyalty and the renewal of our strength through the imparting of His grace. It is all as simple as that. Why should we have all the trappings of a formal service? Why processionals, anthems, chants and responses? Why make the simple so formal? How do we get to God better by indirection than by direction? Accordingly the old time Quakers hold their meetings without set forms. They hold to the value of silence as well as of speech. Communion with this omnipresent Father might be in silence. Exhortation and audible prayer were not ruled out, but one takes his part in the meeting according to what he takes to be the guidance of the Spirit of God. It is believed that the quiet waiting upon God is conducive to the perception of the leadings of the divine Spirit.

An unbiased appraisal of the Quaker meeting would lead to three criticisms, one of the adequacy of the Quaker idea, the other two of practical consequences. In their repudiation of forms the Quakers reject baptism and the Lord's Supper, as it is commonly called. Both practices date from apostolic days. A rule outlawing the communion table appears too stringent. Granted that it has been embellished with high church sacramentarianism it might well be observed as a table of remembrance. Certainly an opportunity to accept baptism and to take communion at the table of the Lord might be presented as optional—not requisite for membership in the group. It is quite arguable to maintain that if Christianity consists of a relationship of the human spirit with the divine Spirit, if it means regeneration, to love God and one's neighbor, "to do justice, love mercy and walk humbly with thy God" then the requirement of compliance with any form as essential to church membership is a contradiction of the nature of Christianity. In this the Quakers are quite consistent. If the optional displaces the required there is no contradiction. To deny the essentiality of any symbol is one thing: to deny its value for some is quite another. The second criticism is voiced by one brought up in Quaker surroundings who upon maturity preferred another church. He objected that the Quaker meeting tended to degenerate into the dryness and inconsequentiality of the average "prayer-meeting." The old fashioned prayer meeting with all its potentialities for good has not shown vitality for survival. It must be admitted that the vast number of churches that have discontinued their midweek meetings have not perceptibly deteriorated spiritually below the level of those that still maintain them. All have attended meetings for prayer and conference that were inspiring, but how often have people with intelligence fretted and those with spiritual sensitiveness groaned under stereotyped speeches reiterating platitudes and prayers that had no lifting power. The third objection may be considered laudatory of the Quaker way, but, nonetheless, is a practical objection. To put it in the most favored manner it is this: relatively few are able to rise to the Quaker ideal. Put in a way less uncomplimentary to church people in general it is the realization that most people are so constituted that they prefer the symbolic. The extenuation of this preference—if it needs excuse—is in the observation already made that Quaker practice scarcely approximates Quaker ideals. In any event a formal service that is beautiful satisfies more than one unencumbered by forms that drag over the dry dust of the inconsequential.

Mention should be made, parenthetically because they are so far from the main stream, of a small and little known sect that aims to reproduce the primitive church and in its practices of worship is similar to the Quakers but retains baptism and the Lord's Supper. They are called Plymouth Brethren because of their origin nearly a century ago in Plymouth, England. They themselves deprecate a sectarian label. They ordinarily refer to themselves as being "in fellowship." Conditions of admittance to their fellowship include strict adherence to fundamentalist views with particular emphasis upon the verbal inspiration and therefore absolute inerrancy of the Bible. They are theologically intolerant and the slightest deviation from accepted dogma is a cause for disciplinary action. In consequence they are themselves very much divided. The principal meetings are those of the "Darbyites" the adherents of Mr. Darby the founder and those of the so-called "Open Brethren". For these reasons they are so separated from other churches that they have little influence upon them as they are little in-influenced by them. Because their worship is a modification of Quaker customs and because they make a sincere attempt to imitate the primitive church they should be included in this discussion. Their uniqueness presents another idea of worship. In contrast with the Quakers and because of their New Testament pattern the observance of the Lord's Supper is a regular part of their weekly worship for the New Testament tells how the early Christians met together "to break bread." Hence with them it is rather the "breaking of bread" than the communion. Although it is so frequently observed it is shorn of all ceremony. At some undesignated time in the course of the Sunday morning meeting some undesignated one will informally reach over to the ordinary table that is in the midst of them, take up in turn the bread and the wine and pass them without remark to the one seated next to him. So they are passed from seat to seat. The last one to partake will replace them on the table. The whole is in conformity with the tone of the meeting which as has been said is after the fashion of the Quakers. The meeting has neither formal beginning nor conclusion. The company assembling in silence continues so until someone announces a hymn, reads the Scriptures or offers prayer. The silent meditation is resumed until someone else is moved to take part. There is no set time for closing, but at approximately the same time each Sunday the meeting will close as it opened without formality. Someone or two or three will rise and the rest will follow. The meeting is ended. The meeting is thus in principle that of the Quakers except for "the breaking of bread." The real difference is here and in the attitudes toward theology. With the Quakers doctrine is relatively unimportant; with the Brethren it is of the utmost importance. They, in contrast to the Quakers, will have nothing to do with regular churches which they consider degenerate. Like some others their ambition is to reproduce the apostolic church in the modern world. So far as their manner of worship is concerned, they probably approach nearer that norm, as they conceive it to be, than others. As a matter of principle all forms may be excluded or made optional; as a matter of practice there is no doubt that the primitive church baptized and observed "the breaking of bread." However the real question is: Do we want to reproduce the apostolic church in our modern world? The earliest Christians were few, mostly humble who had no place in the large world. They were motivated with tremendous enthusiasm that made them zealous to share their spiritual riches with others but they made no apparent impression upon the vast pagan world at least in the earliest phase of their existence. Nor did they expect to. Rather they were inclined to wait in quiet expectation for a messianic return that would wind up mundane affairs. With the missionary expansion there was naturally not only an increase in numbers but a steady increase in influence. But we are far from the primitive days. The centuries have gone by unrolling in their passage a scroll of knowledge and events that have almost incredibly changed the world. Today Christianity

143

has left its fingerprints on numerous lands. Even more than that it has sufficiently gripped certain nations so as to become a formative influence in their lives. If the church has become more worldly in a discreditable sense, it has also become more conscious of its immediate mission to the present world. In the changed circumstances there should be boldness enough to substitute a different norm from that of the church in the first years of the first Christian century. It is possible that imitation might mean stagnation. Our question is not "What should the church do to return to the condition of the primitive?" but "What shall the church do to meet the changed conditions imposed by the modern world?" This applies to its worship as well as to its organization. The answers, as we have seen, are diverse.

Simple logic says with the Quakers of old: "If you want to talk to God, do it. He is here. Pray." Sing if you are in the spirit. Share your experience of God and of the Christian life with other Christians. There is no need of lugging in media of ceremonies that may prove to be an obstruction in the way. Why all this circumlocution? Go directly to God. But in a meeting of a thousand or of thousands such as constitute an occasional church service and often a denominational or interdenominational assembly a Quaker meeting is physically impossible. The gathering is too large. It would be impossible to hear unless each participant went to a microphone. The result would be confusion. It certainly would not be a Quaker meeting. All the dignity, solemnity and beauty would vanish. It would not be practicable to break up a large congregation into small groups each capable of holding its own meeting with proper decorum. It would be uneconomical and would hamper if it did not destroy united service.

The opposite answer is given in terms of liturgy. A crowd here only enhances the impressiveness. This kind of worship as we have seen misses the essential truth in Quaker simplicity. Instead it has developed an approach to God that is fundamentally inconsistent with the Christian conception of God as Father rather than king. It possesses an aesthetic appeal. It is not denied that the aesthetic is related to the spiritual, but it is not to be identified with it. The architecture of the cathedral, the processions of robed choirs and gowned ministers appeals to the eye. The tones of the organ, the voices of the choir, the intonations, it may be, of the minister appeal to the ear. The burning of incense or to a less degree the odor of flowers appeals to the olfactory sense. Bowing and kneeling appeal to the gratification obtained through physical motion. But it is possible to arouse these sensations without any relation to the religion they are supposed to promote. An emotional state with a kind of religious gloss is not religion and may easily be inimical to it. It is well known as a psychological fact that an emotion induced in an atmosphere that is purposely created to make an appeal for responsiveness must find some practical and effective expression or the reaction will be entirely emotional and harmful. Some regard a formal service as cold. It is in reality a service that is filled with emotion, but there is an attempt to direct the emotion, to awaken deep feelings and to yoke all with reason.

The informally crude may be dismissed summarily. It, too, is emotional, but the emotion is connected with reason only by flimsy threads. More often the reason thus remotely connected is really unreason. Its popularity lies in its playing upon familiar and sentimental strings. It thrives upon excitement. The emotions aroused are the strong primitive ones. The defense of it is that it meets people where they are. The objection to it is that it leaves them where they are.

After this survey our conclusion seems barren, our climax weak. But climaxes, except in fiction, are often weak. The purpose of the chapter has been descriptive and analytical; not homiletic. We must disappoint perfectionists, but some constructive ideas emerge from the discussion. The liturgical churches are committed to their ancient ways and are ready with a defense of them. But many free churches are stumblingly seeking light. During the last few years with the revived attention to worship there have been serious studies of the meaning of worship and the programme of worship. A trend has been to re-examine historic liturgies and to maintain the right of all churches to make use of them. The fundamental premise, however, is assumed. It is that the approach to God must be through forms. It seems inexplicable that any possible contribution of the Quakers should be ignored or passed over lightly. Surely silence and meditation in public as well as in private worship have something to offer. The church that takes no account of that is a loser. Some churches have made a place for at least a few moments of silence in their regular order of service. There is also the opportunity for small like-minded groups to meet together from time to time to develop the possibilities latent in the Quaker conception. This would not interfere with the regular church assemblies on Sundays for public worship. Varying ideas are not mutually exclusive.

The more liturgical service has power to stimulate the imagination. The prerogatives of imagination are not to be underestimated. Imagination is the creative artist of the human spirit. It repaints the past as an interpreter of today and furnishes an incentive to greater achievement. It lends color and form to the dull and incoherent present. It unveils a canvas of the future as an inspiration toward progress. Imagination is no menial but a master in the household. Without it there could be no order, no correlation, no hope. Without imagination faith would sputter out like a candle the light of which is extinguished by a harsh wind. And when faith seems cold and dead it is imagination that touches it and causes it to burst out in a new flame. Apart from imagination the wings of poetry are feeble and dull words flutter to the ground. Without imagination science is abashed and defeated and test tube and ruler are in listless hands. Without imagination the home loses its glory as the castles of vision fall. Without imagination education falters for it has lost its goal. Without imagination the farmer foreseeing no harvest discovers no zest for planting. Without imagination industry stops for the finished product no longer pictured fails to supply the incentive of work. It is in religion that imagination obtains a sinister connotation. Religion it is held contemptuously is just imagination—wishful thinking. Religion is not "just imagination" but imagination illuminates religion as it does science, agriculture, industry and all the rest. It is not a word to be tossed aside like a coin that lacks the weight of worth.

The first question about the means of inducing worship is "What images are to be suggested?" Of the king? Of the father? Of the grandeur of the past? Of the realities of the present? Of the blessedness of the future? Of the joy or despair of this world? Of the wonders of the world to come? Of truth, justice, fellowship, love, mercy? There must be a sorting out of possibilities and the adoption of at least some general principles, admitting always that the artist in each individual will have a degree of independence so that all pictures will not be identical. But predetermination is not ruled out. To illustrate: Those who plan the programme of worship may choose between the representation of God as a tyrant who exercises His power to torture those whom He condemns and that of a Savior revealed on a cross.

For examples we might examine and appraise some of the common symbols. Baptism and the Lord's Supper, since they indubitably date from the earliest church, offer themselves for this purpose. Baptism as it is practiced in most churches is, of course, an accommodation of the word and the change in form from immersion to sprinkling has emptied it of symbolic value. Although meaningless in itself, it has been invested with significance by accompanying words. Applied to infants it holds for those who have high church proclivities sacramental value; for others it is really a service of dedication. In respect of adults this baptism in its intrinsic value is vague, but it is hallowed by custom as a ceremonial introduction to a new way of life. It is useful psychologically in that it surrounds the act of Christian affirmation with solemnity and a visible outward expression of self-dedication that makes for a stronger and therefore more indelible impression upon the life. Outward acts have inward effects. Thus baptism has the sentimental sanction of centuries of usage in the larger part of the church and thus has acquired a kind of authoritative influence, but as symbol it has little meaning. The immersionist churches have retained an intelligible symbolism that corresponds with the New Testament explanations of death in Christ to the service of sin and new life in Him. A physician who was a psychiatrist upon being so baptized spoke of it as a memorable experience and one he would not have missed. It is interesting as a comment from such a man of the impression that can be made by an intelligible symbol. Doubtless many feel the same way about it. The spectator may be impressed, too. But in these days the effect produced upon many curious observers is quite different. To them there has been a spectacle that has wrought a revulsion of feeling. The baptized lifted from the waters presents a drenched and bedraggled appearance that is not edifying in the opinion of the less devout and the less approving. Thus a close, critical, impartial consideration of a symbol may lead to unexpected conclusions. Worths cannot be taken for granted. It is not easy to weigh values.

On the other hand the communion table is clear cut in its symbolic meaning. Those who hold all forms in slight regard may consider it superfluous. Even to them, however, the meaning is clear. To partake of the bread and the wine almost inevitably will not only create the idea of fellowship —partakers together of the spirit revealed in Christ—but will turn the imagination back to the scene in the upper room where the Savior sat with his disciples and broke the bread and passed the cup. The solemnity, the sacrifice, the beauty of that scene will unfold before the mind. The imagination will follow Jesus to the hill of Calvary and the meditations evoked will be of "wonder, love and praise." New resolution will crystallize in the mind and will. These effects will be produced irrespective of theological concepts and of sacramental evaluations. Thus there can be a fairly definite prediction of the effect upon the thoughtful and devout worshiper when he comes to the communion table. We know not only that the imagination will be stirred, but what pictures will be formed by it.

The symbolism of the cross is also definite. It can have but one central meaning although the individual imagination may enrich that with many colors supplied by the palette of the particular artist within the soul. There may be not only the vision of the cross but also a vision of the experience of the worshiper with its sins and shames; the peace and joy of forgiveness. There may be such amplifications, but the central theme and its meaning remain constant.

The concentration of a few moments upon the open Bible in the pulpit may entice the imagination to conduct a tour through scenes of unsurpassed magnificence. One is taken into the remote past. Abraham is seen leaving his country to go upon his pilgrimage of faith. One sees not only the herds, the pastures, the encampments, but a primitive spirit of responsiveness to God. One sees Moses living in the splendors of Egyptian palaces, but renouncing the life of ease and casting his lot with his own people. One catches the far away look in his eyes as he stands upon the mountain amid the flashes of lightning and the roll of thunder striving to understand the law of God. One sees David the shepherd lad, the harpist soothing the disturbed mind of King Saul, sees David the exile, the conquering king, the broken-hearted father. The pages of Israel's history pass before the mind—wicked Ahab and intrepid Elijah, the good Josiah borne in his chariot into his capital defeated and dead. One sees the prophets—Isaiah in the temple overwhelmed by his vision of divine glory, Jeremiah pleading, weeping, persecuted, Ezekiel and his idealistic visions of a grandeur that shall be, Amos looking across the desert from Tekoa and going forth without fear to denounce royal apostasy in the king's own sanctuary, Micah the peasant championing the cause of the poor and dispossessed, Hosea in his domestic trouble that disclosed to him divine patience and love. The tour continues through the New Testament. The scenes of the life of Jesus are reconstructed. He is alone upon the mountain of temptation. He is wearied at the well of Sychar. He reaches out His hand to the leper. He preaches in the synagogues. He fascinates the multitude with His simple, homely stories. He opens His heart to His friends. He rides in lowly triumph into Jerusalem. He enters the shadows of Gethsemane. He is shrouded in the darkness of the cross. He emerges into the light of a new life. There are new lands to be visited through the Acts of the Apostles. A church is established in faith, hope and power. Peter and John bestow their benediction sweet indeed because of their close acquaintance with Jesus upon earth. Paul proceeds from land to land proclaiming the gospel, founding churches. The new religion spreads. There are conflicts with political as well as religious authority. Paul, though as a prisoner, reaches Rome the capital of the World. There is a series of letters most of them from the pen of Paul. They describe the spiritual grandeur of Jesus; His heavenly preeminence. The letters glow with the pictures of the idealism of a Christian community, churches and individual Christians, imperfect, struggling against their own simple proclivities, persecuted but unawed by the threatening predominance of paganism, feeling their way in this unaccustomed condition of Christian teaching and its implications for everyday life, aspiring to further spiritual attainments, serving those within their fellowship and eagerly stretching forth hands in helpfulness to those without. As a climax to the journey we are conducted into the mysterious symbolism of the Apocalypse. There is a mingling of opposites: the slain lamb and the lion of the tribe of Judah; vials of wrath and assuaged grief; scrolls of judgment and a volume of redemption; a bottomless pit and an eternal city. Above all, the vision of this eternal city has been the inspiration of the faithful, the city with its gates of pearl, its streets of gold, its cleansing fountain, its trees of healing, its freedom from sin and death and its perpetual light. The pictures of Revelation may not all harmonize with the portrait of the Savior on the cross, but the purport of it all is clear. The hearts of persecuted believers are cheered and their courage established with the assurance that the Lord of love is also the Lord of life, that the Savior of men whom they may approach without fear is to be sovereign having conquered the forces of evil. Most appropriately the journey with imagination as guide reaches its climax when there is displayed the magnificence of the celestial city. The Bible has become a symbol of a stirring faith.

The architecture of a church is symbolic and lights the torch of imagination. The gothic arch, as everyone knows, is a symbol of the upward look and the aspiration for the heavenly. Church windows if they are not, as unhappily they often are in non-liturgical churches, either grotesque or crude may stimulate a devout imagination.

The symbol should exercise some control over the imagination it excites. Imagination is not like a forest where one without a compass goes circling about getting nowhere. On the contrary it must be a path to reality.

The pure symbol is to be distinguished from form. The one appeal of the symbol is to imagination. The form is a more direct approach to God through worship. It may have some power to create an image. In that sense it utilizes qualities of imagination. Avoiding any reiteration of the controversy between the respective values of set forms and of spontaneity in worship we limit our consideration to whether forms are prescribed and unalterable or variable and free from all ecclesiastical imposition. The test of any form used in worship is its adequacy and effectiveness in producing the desired impression and inducing the desired attitude upon the part of the worshiper. If, for illustration, we are adapting the purpose of leading the congregation into the presence of a Father who is merciful toward them as sinners, compassionate with them as burdened with infirmities and sorrows, supplying grace for daily struggles, revitalizing their aspirations, inviting them to be workers with Him in seeking to establish truth, justice, love in the present world—a Father who is revealed supremely in Jesus Christ—then our question is "How do the forms we use succeed in this purpose?" Every part of worship should be scrutinized to see if it fulfills its mission.

We may carry our inquiry further by asking what should be the proportion and indeed the relation of the direct and the indirect in a service of worship? The congregational singing, the "general confession" in which all join are examples of the direct since they obviously constitute a direct approach to God in prayer—sung or spoken. A hymn is really a prayer set to music. The elements in the words of a hymn are the same as the elements in a spoken prayer: praise, confession, aspiration, dedication. The music of the organ may serve as an illustration of the indirect. In its appeal to emotion and imagination in its suggestion of harmony, it may produce a worshipful attitude upon the part of the auditors. Whatever answer there may be to the question—indeed all the questions—we have raised it is not found in the formulation of any rule. Ideas of public worship are too diverse for that. All that may be hoped is for the provision of material for the construction of an answer —or of answers. This material must be gathered from pondering these aspects of a programme of worship and the contents that we have been considering. There must be a realization that a service of worship is not composed of hymns, prayers, readings, anthems, thrown together so that none of the conventional parts shall be missing. Nor is it sufficient to attain a numerical proportion of these diverse parts and to join them with a certain regard for congruity and smoothness. Thoughtless imitation of some traditional way that commends itself by reason of dignity and beauty will not do. Materials of worship must be used within the framework of an adequate conception of what worship is in respect of its definition and purpose.

We began this chapter with a simple explanation of worship as a means of making contact with God. We may appropriately conclude it by considering the effects that worship are designed to produce in the worshiper. The shaping of an "order of worship" will depend upon this also. Worship like the Christian religion in its wholeness is for the entire personality. The emotions, the intellect, the will should be integrated. Emotion without intelligence is dangerous. Intellect alone is unproductive. There can be no worthful course of action by sheer voluntariness. It needs the generating power of emotional fire and the directing power of intelligence. The ultimate that we are seeking is not conduct for conduct is an expression of something deeper in the life. To use common language and avoid the exactitudes of psychological definitions what we are trying to induce in religion generally and in worship specifically is right feeling. That is the real fundamental. Jesus compressed his teaching into two great precepts: love God and love your neighbor. That we shall give God the loyalty and affection of children to a good father is the natural, the inevitable result of the Christian gospel. The human application is similar but different. It should not be hard to love a kind father. It is hard to love an unkind neighbor. But that is religion. Worship that does not induce kindly feelings toward undeserving men falls lamentably short of its purpose. He who comes from the sanctuary with benevolence toward his fellows has not worshipped in vain. It is he who has not stood complacently or with indifferent convention in the outer court but has entered the most holy place. It is he who has worshipped God in spirit and in truth. Conduct? Appropriate right action springs as naturally from such feelings as flowers from the rich and well watered soil of a garden.

Chapter VI

THE ECUMENICAL CHURCH

It is sometimes said that sectarianism is the great sin of Protestantism. Of course it is not. A few moments thought should convince anyone that other sins, like unbrotherliness, are far greater. Diversity is both the penalty and the reward of freedom. While it cripples effectiveness, it enriches experience. In our religion there are many contributions. Blended they could be of much value. To what extent can they be blended? It is the nature of Protestantism to allow —even to encourage—divisions. Yet it is true enough that denominational cleavages are offensive. There is something repugnant about the variety of denominational signboards that decorate church edifices. Admitting that diversity is unavoidable is it necessarily and in all respects prohibitive of unity? Nowadays many of our divisions are unreal. Baptists serve Presbyterian churches. Methodists are at home in Congregational pulpits. Denominations unite for specific purposes and on special occasions. During recent years denominations that had much in common have discovered bases for union. So, for example, the Congregational and Christian churches have amalgamated. The Church of Canada is an illustration just across our borders of union upon a larger scale. More recently India has furnished an example to America, to all Christendom—of the most extensive amalgamation of denominations that we have seen. In south India the new church includes Anglican, Congregational, Presbyterian, Methodist, Reformed churches. It will be noted that the union is not complete. Baptists who have had a notable history in south India did not join in the movement. A looser but practically efficient federation of denominations was made possible when the Federal Council of Churches was formed in the United States. The basis of federation was broadly evangelical. The parent organization of the National Council formulated pronouncements of the member churches in public affairs, in social and economic relations and directed united plans for evangelism. Even here there are denominations that have stood aloof or even in opposition. The largest body of dissidents has been the southern Baptists. Respecting denominational differences the National Council has promoted a sense of fundamental Christian unity in principle and in practice.

In 1948 the most ambitious scheme of inter-church fellowship and co-operation was consummated in the formation of the World Council of Churches. This geographically as well as denominationally comprehensive organization was an attempt to acknowledge that not only Protestant but Orthodox churches had much in common and to furnish a means for the expression of Christian principles and the recognition of an approximately universal fellowship. The World Council is not universal. The Roman Catholic Church was not represented officially at Amsterdam, where the first meeting was held, although there were Catholic observers present. Sundry fundamentalist groups would have no part in it. It is at an enormous distance from a universal church.

The more recent meeting of the World Council in Evanston in 1954 records little advance in ecumenicity. The subject chosen for the conference "Christ the Hope of the World" stirred disagreements and did not augment the spirit of unity except as it was shown to be possible to discuss subjects, about which opinions differ, in an amicable fashion. That is something that might be considered practical and important. Undoubtedly the topic did stir up a diversity of views. Some connected the hope with a literal return of Christ; to others it connoted social evolution. And there were opinions between such extremes. These discussions seemed a digression from the primary object of the Council which is to develop areas of agreement and furnish some evidence of the essential unity of the differing churches all insisting that they are Christian.

The World Council of Churches with all its inclusiveness is limited to a small area of co-operation. The National Council has a much larger area, but it distinctly respects denominational organizations and finds its considerable strength through its refusal to interfere in denominational differences and its concentration upon objectives common to all. Those—and of course they are many—who are zealous for church union, impatient of seemingly interminable delays and circuitous routes opened a direct road in December 1949. A conference was held in Greenwich, Connecticut where there gathered representatives of Methodist, Presbyterian, U.S.A., Disciples of Christ, Congregational Christian, Evangelical and Reformed, Colored Methodist Episcopal, African Methodist Episcopal, Zion churches to consider positive church union. The conference perpetuated itself through committees. The importance of this Conference on Church Union lies in the fact that it is definitely working toward its appointed task. It must be noted that churches not negligible in numbers or influence were not represented. Nevertheless the movement was on an unprecedented scale.

All of these movements represent a stirring of the Christian conscience, a groping for at least a tenuous fellowship and a recognition that the world requires the impact of something in the semblance of united Christian witness to save it from ruin. Circumstances are forcing the churches together. What should be the goal of those who believe that the perpetuation of differences that once were living but now are dead or moribund is folly, perhaps sin? Uniformity

157

in all respects is out of the question. To ban diversity would be to stifle life. The aim clearly is to seek unity— that will allow diversity and diversity that will not exclude union.

Certain boundaries must be accepted however regretfully. There are generally speaking three areas separated from each other by mountains of difference that cannot be scaled. The first is that of extreme fundamentalism. The second is that of extreme sacramentarianism. The third is that of evangelical, free Christianity.

Fundamentalism is the outgrowth of one root so stubborn that it cannot be eradicated. Without understanding this, fundamentalism cannot be understood. The root is the tenacious and uncompromisable belief that the Bible is verbally inspired. Any deviation from this idea is never so slight as to be negligible. To the fundamentalist the Bible in its original text is the inerrant Word of God. For most fundamentalists it is as if God dictated to human stenographers that which He would have them transcribe and the stenographers themselves were protected from the errors to which stenographers are prone. The reason that genuine fundamentalists cannot tolerate any deviation from the belief in literally inspired Scriptures is that it would be repudiation of their final authority, the Word of God. Whatever criticisms may be leveled against so-called liberals for unorthodox conception of the incarnation of Jesus or the atonement or any scepticism about the bodily resurrection of Jesus can be reduced to simplest terms—rejection of a verbally inspired Bible. Fundamentalists believe that to support churches, ministers and missionaries who do not agree with this view of the Bible is disloyalty to the faith "once for all delivered to the saints." The only condition upon which fundamentalists will have fellowship or co-operation with liberals even within a denomination is that the liberal group shall acquiesce in fundamentalist principles and policies. Their continuance in a denomination that is theologically divided is contingent upon a belief in their ability to induce the acceptance of their ideas and practices. While hope continues of eventually gaining control they may remain within struggling perpetually for dominance. If that is gained they will adopt such a creed as will force all dissidents to withdraw rather than consent to it. If the fundamentalists were in control the more direct way would be to exclude from the denomination those who do not agree with them. This is really superfluous for the end is more easily gained by the indirect method. In certain denominations that are not notably liberal, the Presbyterian and Baptist for instance, the fundamentalists have seceded and formed organizations of their own.

Fundamentalists are not to be confused with conservatives who may hold views that closely approach those of fundamentalists. In general this group may profess ideas of scriptural inspiration approximating those of the fundamentalists but they do not believe that their opinion compels them to separate themselves from other Christians who disagree with them. It cannot be denied that modern times have produced disagreements and confusion in the churches especially because of altered views of Scriptural inspiration. It is not the difference in views that counts, but the importance attached to identity of belief. Since fundamentalists insist that adherence to the authority of an infallible Bible is essential to Christianity it is evident that no plan for unity of churches could be devised that would not be rejected by them as repugnant and a surrender of faith. It is therefore obvious that they are excluded by their intransigence from any plan for a united church. They will have nothing to do with it. Instead they will go to great lengths to set obstacles in its way. In any free society they must be allowed to continue as separatists. To that extent the ecumenical hope is beyond realization. With the fundamentalists must

be classed other groups that may be antipodal in their thinking from them but who are so far from evangelical Christianity that they reject whatever faith is held in common by
the churches. Such, for example, are the Christian Scientists
whose name is conclusive evidence that they consider themselves Christians but whose teachings are incompatible with
both historical Christianity or what today is generally known
as evangelical Christianity. At best it is a hybrid variety
accepting certain Christian principles but substituting for
the Christianity represented by Catholics as well as Protestants claims to truth that would warrant classification as
that of a distinct religion. Classification and names put aside
as irrelevant it would be unthinkable that groups of this
sort could merge in any organization that bore a semblance
to Christianity in its accepted connotation. Thus to begin we
eliminate a rather numerous portion of our religious community that uses the name Christian properly or erroneously
and is classed as Protestant as distinct at least from Roman
Catholic.

Another section of the Christian church must be considered as irreconcilables and therefore offering little or
no hope of unity. This consists of the Sacramentarians. The
most conspicuous of these are in the Protestant Episcopal
Church as we have seen. They are fundamentalists of a
different sort. They may hold modern opinions about the
Bible. That is not important to them for it is not a book
of final authority. The final authority for them is in the
church. That is fundamental in their religious conception.
They believe that power was given to the church by its
Lord and that through the sacraments of the church men
enter into salvation. There is a little elasticity in this view.
They see men and women like the Quakers the genuineness
of whose Christianity nobody questions. The churchmen
often being mild, kindly and thoroughly Christian in spirit
cannot consign such people to outer darkness. Even the

160

Roman Catholic church that claims exclusive possession of the keys to the doors of salvation leaves apertures through which non-Catholics may squeeze in. But the regularly appointed way is sacramental. However, no informed person would allege that an appropriate inwardness of spirit is not presupposed in the efficacy of sacraments.

The position of the ritualist is this: he argues that we live in a physical world where there is an unavoidable interrelation between the physical and the spiritual. Man is primarily a spirit, but the spirit expresses itself through the body. So it is maintained God uses the physical as a vehicle for the spiritual. In order that salvation may be ministered to man God has ordained certain visible means. God's grace is communicated through the rites. It is that which gives sacramental value to them. In this scheme of things baptism is the medium of saving grace. It is more than a symbol. It has actual value in itself. Similarly the communion table is not just a memorial of the last supper. It is a means of imparting grace. The sacraments are generally indispensable means for this ministration of spiritual power. The churchman may not countenance an evasion of them. This insistence upon ritual does not exclude direct communion of the Spirit of God with the human spirit. Witness the mystics, some of whom are canonized in the Roman Catholic church.

Furthermore sacraments must be properly administered. Since this is the prerogative of the church it is the church alone that can confer power upon her chosen priests for this office. Authority is said to have been conferred by Jesus upon his apostles and upon them alone. They, in turn, had the power to pass on this authority to others by ordination to the ministry of the church. Again it must be understood that ordination is not mere recognition of a call to certain functions, but the bestowal of actual power. Hence it is necessary generally to secure the validity of the administration of the sacraments by the validity of ordination. Otherwise the whole churchly structure falls apart. This explains the familiar phrase "apostolic succession." Those ordained by the church are recipients of authority derived from God and bestowed upon the apostles who in unbroken succession through the Christian ages have conferred this authority upon others.

This conviction of the ritualist in respect of sacraments and apostolic succession is based first upon inferences from Scriptures that tell how Jesus gave keys to the kingdom to Simon Peter and how others were ordained to fill the apostolic ranks depleted by the treachery of Judas Iscariot along with such injunctions about ordaining "bishops or elders" as came from the pen of the apostle Paul. The Scriptures are supplemented by tradition. It is through tradition that the claims of unbroken succession from the apostolic times are set forth. The Episcopal church or more accurately its Anglo-Catholic party holds strongly to the trustworthiness of tradition. Its position is that tradition unrefuted by history has a strong claim to credence. Tradition often is the fiber from which history is woven. It is triumphantly pointed out that the church preceded the New Testament by some years and therefore the contention that the New Testament is the authority for the church and the Christian is demonstrably false. The New Testament came from the church, not the church from the New Testament. One fact, however, is overlooked. That fact renders inconclusive the reasoning of the high churchman. It is that Christianity preceded the church. The church as an institution had no existence before the day of Pentecost according to the New Testament record. Weeks passed from the time of the cross and the triumph of Jesus over death before Pentecost. During this time there was a community of believers. There were the apostles and, we are told, that others believed on Jesus. The three alleged facts upon which Christianity is founded had all come into being: the coming of Jesus,

162

ordinarily called the incarnation, the death of Jesus, ordinarily designated as the atonement, and the re-emergence of the crucified Christ known as the resurrection. Nothing essential has been added through the Christian centuries to these three foundation stones. Unorganized and inchoate as it may have been there was a group of Christians without either New Testament or church. Of course the authority was in neither, but in the Spirit of God manifested in a new way it may be at Pentecost, but not at that time making a first contact with men. The Spirit of God guide and authority from the beginning was the authority for the Christian. But whatever may be argued about priorities the high churchman is adamant in his insistence upon the spiritual primacy of the church. A host of Episcopalians are not to be included —certainly not completely—under the same category as the Anglo-Catholics many of whose ways are abhorrent to them. They have little faith in the reliability of the tradition that makes the doctrine of apostolic succession possible. Some scoff at the flimsiness of the evidence for such a doctrine. These do not belong to the company of the intransigents. But what prospects there are of wooing thorough-going sacramentarians from their uncompromising attitude are less than microscopic. Not that they oppose church unity. Many of them are strongly committed to it, but always on their own terms. In other words, they are willing to receive the erring into the true fold. Their fundamental convictions compel them to this immovability. They must be eliminated from considerations in respect of ecumenicity unless the other churches are willing to surrender their convictions. An illustration is furnished by the union achieved in South India. It included, as will be remembered, the Anglican church established there. The new church has met with strong opposition from Anglo-Catholics although it would seem to the neutral observer that the plan in South India was a decided concession to the Episcopal view. At the assembly for the consummation of the union the ministers of all the uniting churches were accepted through the acknowledgment and commissioning of both the Episcopal and non-Episcopal churches. The ministers of the non-Episcopal churches stood and were commissioned by the bishop of the Anglicans. Apparently this did not involve the laying on of Episcopal hands. It did mean a new and distinct commission from Episcopal authorities. But new applicants for the ministry were set apart by the bishop. Then there was conveyed whatever power might be considered resident in Episcopal consecration. If there was any lapse at all in the transmission of authority believed inherent in the doctrine of apostolic succession it was temporary and would terminate with the lives of those non-Episcopalians accepted at the time that the union was formed. If even a transient deviation from the norm established in the Church of England is disapproved by the high church party, as it is, it is an unavoidable inference that ecumenicity can be achieved only on the terms of surrender to a conception of Christianity that is repugnant to a very large part of Christendom.

There are churches like the Quakers and Baptists that are unalterably committed to an anti-sacramental view of Christianity. There are others like the Presbyterians who are not sacramentarian but who still call the Lord's Supper a sacrament. Baptists would call it only an ordinance. But it is safe to say that a member of a Presbyterian church who expressed disbelief in the Lord's Supper as a sacrament would not be excluded from the church because of his disbelief or even be subjected to discipline.

The convictions of the "free" churches are that religion must not be identified with a form. To them that is theoretically untenable and practically dangerous. Redemption they maintain is a purely spiritual process. Men are not condemned because of failure to conform to any rite that is external, for salvation is solely a matter of the spirit. Baptismal regeneration is generally repudiated these days even by churches that speak of the sacrament of baptism. It is mostly a matter of semantics. Failure to comply with any form however sacred its associations cannot affect the religious position of any man. Practically history has made us keenly aware of the ease with which the rite usurps and becomes sole occupant of the throne of authority. It is easier to do some external thing however hard forgetting the spiritual exercise that theoretically is supposed to accompany it than it is to force one's self to a thorough spiritual purgation as the sole means of the benefits desired. It avoids, too, that concentration of thought and inward examination and determination that people would rather escape. Thus this radical Protestantism is on the opposite side of the religious world to that of sacramentarianism.

The thorough Protestant has this different conception of sacraments. He believes that all the experiences of life that come from God are sacramental. There is the sacrament of work. God touches us in our daily labor. If it becomes, as it may, a means of imparting grace it is a sacrament certainly. There is the sacrament of play. If we break "recreation" into its two component parts and think of "re-creation" play obviously is sacramental. There is the sacrament of friendship. If in the love of a friend we find evidences of divine love and feel that it is imparted to us in friendship, surely that qualifies it to be considered sacramental. There is even the sacrament of sorrow. Many a soul has raised a Bethel through grief because sorrow has been a means of contact with the Heavenly Father. Why should sacraments be limited to a few customs sanctioned by ecclesiastical authorities? There are those who discover God's grace more in the first flowers of the springtime, the song of the hermit thrush, the caress of a child, the clasp of a hand than in the communion table. Surely we may not expel them from our Christian community. But, if we don't, we shatter our traditional conception of sacraments. It is only fair to make a practical distinction between, for example, the Lord's Supper and the kind of experience described. The traditionally designated sacraments of the church have definite associations. They may be the association of the events commemorated such as the baptism of Jesus and the Last Supper and also the association of the generations of Christians that have observed these practices. It is, therefore, altogether defensible to retain these observances. To set them up as possessing particular sacramental value is a quite different matter.

If a person or a group makes the "sine qua non"—the indispensable prerequisite for church union either the acceptance of a verbally inspired Bible or the doctrine of apostolic succession and the sacramental interpretation of Christianity it is indisputable that those who cannot honestly agree are excluded from admission into the "true" church. As supplement, corollary or further explanation it may be noted that in general where the condition of union is that the dissenter must surrender and join an organization that claims sole possession of essential truth that condition is not an obstacle to ecumenicity that may conceivably be overcome but a partition that effectively and permanently separates. It is strange that ardent advocates of church union have slurred over these irreconcilable divisions and have failed to draw the unavoidable conclusion that in any contemplated joining of Protestant forces there are these large areas that make any approximation of complete union impossible.

After we have taken a cool calculation of these facts, there remains in our sight a great body of Protestants to whose union obstacles are not insuperable.

Our consideration should begin at the points already softened enough for fusion. Practically there is today an

166

interchange of membership among denominations. A recent calendar of a Congregational church contained a list of new members. Most of them were from Baptist or Methodist churches. That is typical. Numerous Baptist churches have open or associate membership whereby this formerly exclusive denomination accepts members of other evangelical churches into its own membership regardless of baptismal requirements that once were absolute. Almost any evangelical church will have on its roll names of men and women who have changed their denomination without having changed or, they believe, compromised their views. Ministers of various denominations are not aware of any sectarian barrier to fullness of friendship, association, worship, service. A Presbyterian, Congregationalist, Baptist minister will not feel the least an alien in a Methodist pulpit nor will he be treated as such. The fact is that denominational divisions have little or no meaning to most Protestants. This is partly because of ignorance of what were once considered denominational principles, partly because of indifference to them, partly because there is a feeling that denominational demarcations have been practically erased. What denominational convictions remain are held by only a few. For the most part even such denominational loyalty is like that of a student to his school.

The best starting place for a project in unity for the various sects is the practical one. It has often been remarked that we worship together and serve together. Since that constitutes most of practical religion it means considerable. The hymn books are notably non-sectarian. They contain hymns written by Unitarians, Presbyterians, Methodists, Episcopalians and all the rest not excluding Roman Catholics. Cardinal Newman's "Lead Kindly Light" is a general favorite. So is Father Faber's "Faith of Our Fathers." Strangely enough the "Kindly Light" led Newman into Roman Catholicism and the "Faith of Our Fathers" ex-

167

tolled by Father Faber is that of the Roman Catholic church. These facts do not prevent the lusty singing of the hymns by the most ardent evangelicals.

Consider some of the fences that separate church from church. Perhaps they are not immovable.

Begin with organizations. The differences range from episcopacy to local congregational government. In a previous chapter we challenged the authority for us of the apostolic church in worship. We may broaden our challenge. First of all it would be a good exercise for us to strip our minds of the notion that it is our business to reproduce the primitive church in any respect: that the primitive church must be perpetuated in all its primitiveness. Of course most of those who accept the apostolic church as their model are inconsistent in that they allow women to speak in their meetings and pray with their heads uncovered. There are a few minor sects that cling to these prohibitions and try to preserve the practice of speaking with tongues. Whatever that may mean it was probably something different from the artificial exhibitions of those who would imitate it. Yet even those churches read the gospels. The apostolic church did not for the simple reason that the gospels were not written then. The obvious truth carried by the New Testament narrative is that the ideas of the earliest church were inchoate. The really primitive church had no deacons. It seems reasonably clear that the organization of the church developed according to growing needs. When deacons were required the church organized itself sufficiently to elect them. Our task is not to copy the primitive church but to learn a lesson plainly taught by it. The lesson is that the organization of the church may expand and adapt itself to conditions. Thus episcopacy as the recognition of a doctrine establishing ecclesiastical and priestly authority is one thing—episcopacy as the best means for performing the task of the modern church is quite another. The question can be examined from the point of view of efficiency. Is it the best means or is it not?

Immediately we expect a clash with those who hold strongly for congregationalism—the power of the local church—as a conviction. Here as elsewhere we are told that there must be no compromise with principle. What is meant is that there must be no compromise with prejudice. In this instance the historical foundation is insecure and the logical superstructure is flimsy. What was a local church in New Testament times? The apostle Paul wrote a letter to the church in Rome. How many assemblies of Christians were there in that city when the apostle wrote? Who knows? Could two or more assemblies be separate churches for some functions, worship, for example, and unite as one church for other functions, legislation for example? What historically was the local church and how was it sacrosanct? The contention that no outside authority bishop, assembly or convention may compel a local church to obey its edicts rests upon the contention that the Spirit of God is not to be confined in His direction to any hierarchical or delegated body. The principle may be true, but the logic of it demands unanimous instead of majority decisions in every local church. For if a local church should not take orders from any outside body neither should an individual Christian take orders from the local church. Only the Quakers seek unanimity and they not always successfully for there have been divisions among them. As a matter of practical expediency in democracy we have accepted the dictum "The majority rules." The individual usually acquiesces. He is at liberty to withdraw from the church as a protest. He may refuse his co-operation in a cause in which he does not believe. For example a church may vote money to a cause of which he does not approve and he may give his money with the stipulation that none shall be used for that particular purpose. None can control the individual Christian

169

or the individual church. In general the vote of the majority is accepted although everyone knows the minority may be right. The minority may continue its efforts to change the policy it disapproves. Time may vindicate one side or the other. Why does local geography make a difference in acquiescence to the rule of the majority? As a matter of necessary convenience in a democracy that is larger than the New England town meeting some authority must be delegated to representatives of the larger body of voters. It is so in our United States government where representatives in Congress have the power to make laws under a constitution that both protects minorities and sets up the limiting frame work under which Congress may act. Baptists who are most democratically minded have long accepted this necessary principle of co-operation. A local church or an individual may refuse to accept the action of a body in which the local church is represented by delegates, but in general there is an acceptance of the acts of the larger body. In any such convention or assembly there are motions made that are hotly debated. Take as illustration the sets of resolutions characteristic of any religious body. Almost always there are resolutions on the attitude of the church toward public affairs; almost always is there debate and disagreement about the adoption of the resolutions. They seldom express the opinion or conviction of all the delegates. When they are adopted they are sent out to the world as representing the attitude of the denomination voting them. Although there may be many who disagree with some of the resolutions adopted they will be accepted as expressing the ideas of the majority. The minority may continue in its disbelief and continue to give utterance to its dissent, but it is highly unlikely that dissension will mean secession. Our conception of democracy demands that there shall be no legislation without representation. Granted that, we still are compelled by practical necessity to accept the decisions of the meeting in which we were represented by delegates. Here, too, as in our national government restrictions may be written into the fundamental law. There may be some things a representative assembly may not do.

The defensible and understandable fear of the authority of an extraneous body is deeply rooted in the life of independent churches. The power of the Roman Catholic hierarchy is an ever present example and warning. But Roman Catholicism is not democratic. Protestantism is democratic. Again thinking practically this fear is largely a bogey. In Protestantism there is only a theoretical danger that the local church or the individual conscience will be coerced. Methodism is the largest Protestant denomination in the United States to have what may be called an Episcopal form of government. But does anyone suppose that a Methodist bishop will succeed in defying the desires of a local church? In the first place no sensible bishop—and may we not universalize that and say that the bishops are reasonably sensible?—will try to force his will upon a local church. In theory he has the authority to assign pastors to churches. In general Methodist churches accept the pastors appointed—after all the appointment is up for reconsideration in a year—because they believe in the practical advantages of the system. But it is the habit of the bishop to try to learn the wishes of the churches. If a church objects to an appointment there will probably be some conference. If this does not bring agreement and the church persists in its refusal to receive the pastor assigned the bishop will think more than twice before he attempts to force the church to obey him.

The Protestant Episcopal Church is apparently committed at least as much as any other denomination to the Episcopal system of government. But not only is the bishop limited in his rule by canon law, it is also true that he will not ignore the wishes of the church and impose decisions contrary to its expressed desires. In a rather recent case the decision of the bishop was challenged and an appeal was taken to the civil courts. It is evidence that the episcopal authority may be questioned by the local church or its vestrymen. In the particular case it should be added the bishop was not trying to over-ride the wish of the church, but really discover what the wish of the church was. It was a divided church and things in general were so mixed that it was difficult to decide what the church wanted. Though the government in an Episcopal church is not congregational the governing boards are democratically elected. The ultimate authority practically rests with the congregation. The church will select its own minister.

In these days of democracy there is not much reason for fear of the imposition of external authority. If we accept the conclusion that seems to be both historically and logically warranted that there is no copy-plate form of church that must be reproduced in all ages, but that organization is free and adaptable to changing needs, the differences of opinion about ecclesiastical government ought not to be insuperable obstacles toward agreement among the churches that do not belong either to extreme fundamentalistic or extreme episcopal groups. Convictions would not be challenged if on the ground of practical advantage a plan of government were formulated. It might use bishops without any doctrine of apostolic succession which very many Episcopalians with clear eyes for history do not take too seriously, or set up presbyteries or decide upon congregationalism. Indeed if the projected union was not closely woven various forms could exist together in a federation that would abolish denominational titles and unite in world service.

We turn back to the question of worship. There is already considerable variety in churches of the same denomination. Certainly it is hard to pick two Congregational, Presbyterian or Baptist churches that are precisely the same in their conduct of worship. Advantages of conformity to one norm are negligible. At the present time, too, we sit about the communion table with divergent views of what it means. Some emphasize a sacramental value that they believe and feel inheres in it. Some minimize that sacramental value. Some deny it entirely. It is to them a form perhaps superfluous in which they join as a symbol of fellowship. This condition, let it be repeated, actually prevails now. If there were a fusion of churches there would be no change whatever. If communion were voluntary, not compulsory, Christians could participate without committing themselves to any theory.

What of baptism? There differences of belief are revealed by action. In this respect there is dissimilarity to the communion service where participation does not in the least express the underlying meaning held by the participant. Sprinkling is conspicuously different from immersion. The baptism of an infant is visibly a departure from the Baptist affirmation of "believer's baptism." But what if the Baptists perceive that logically they are committed to the unessentiality of forms? To them, then, forms would not be a cause of contention unless compliance with them became compulsory. Within the same church there would be a policy of inclusiveness that would admit immersion for those who desired it, sprinkling for those who preferred it and simple confession of faith without baptism for those who consider forms a hindrance and not a help. Similarly a difference of opinion between those who hold to believer's baptism—that is that confession of faith as expression of religious experience and decision should precede baptism —and those who adhere to the custom of baptizing infants need not become divisive. Children, that is infants even, may be dedicated to God and the church with the committal of the parent to a religious rearing of the children. It is not a matter of primary importance whether or not water should be used. If there is agreement that baptism is not a means of salvation a few drops of water will do no harm nor will the absence of water vitiate the meaning. Those who are insistent in drawing theological inferences will contend that it is not so simple, that it concerns the very idea of the church. Does the church consist of believers or believers and their children? If we tear off fusty phraseology there is less room for drastic dispute. Actually Protestant churches consist of enrolled members and, in general, the names of children who have made no confession of faith are not inscribed. What then is the practical difference? The pedo-Baptist who makes the purely theoretical claim of believer's children as included in the church will not argue that a child who through no fault of his own has been born in a non-Christian home is regarded by God as separated from Him while a child through no merit of his own who is born in a Christian home is therefore in God's favor. If, given the definition of God's nature generally accepted in Protestantism, there were any difference it would plainly be in God's especial mercy toward the unfortunate child. Any other idea would be an insult to God. What is actually meant in these days when baptismal regeneration is repudiated is the plain factual condition. The child reared in a Christian home and brought up in the Christian church has an obvious advantage in a very practical way. We may leave the metaphysical considerations out of the account. God and the church have a claim upon all childhood. Only where children are brought to the church by their parents is this claim made valid in practice. Since the membership represented on the church roll consists exclusively of those who have confessed their faith what if some should hold one theory and others another about the definition of the church? When the ideas are scrutinized as we have attempted to scrutinize them there is little room for argument.

Creedal differences need not be separative when opinions

are held in other than a bigoted spirit. It seems safe to say that no two people think exactly alike. Diversities of belief are found not only in the same denomination, but in the same local church. This is an existent fact. Unification would not create then what already is. It is true that there must be some basic harmony of thought. There is a rather general understanding of what Christianity really is. It can be stated without equivocation that it is theistic, that Jesus is central in its life, that the Bible is the supreme book of religion, that life is not limited to the present world but extends beyond and that the supreme motive in life should be love. There have been historic creeds—with which many do not agree. The "apostles' creed" is retained and read as part of the worship in some churches; discarded in others. Some who are advocates of its retention believe in it only as an historic statement of Christian beliefs subject to modern interpretations that to the ordinary person look like repudiations of its plain statements. Even the World Council affirmation that Christ is God is open to sundry interpretations. There are staunch supporters of this new world movement toward ecumenicity who do not accept the statement in its apparent meaning. They would agree only that Christ is God in the sense that the Spirit of God governed Him supremely. In short it must be evident that church unity cannot come through creeds. Certainly all churches have some basic creed. It is not necessarily a written one or even formulated in any strict sense. There must be some common ground of belief. The real objection to a creed comes when it is turned into a condition for worship or service. A free expression of faith is quite different from the imposition of a creedal statement. There would be an epidemic of spiritual writers' cramp when the time for signing names to any creed arrived.

With creeds as with other disagreements there could and should be faith in the conquest of truth among Christian

175

people all of whom confess to docility of spirit, a willingness to be taught by God. Let opposing ideas fight it out in an arena of tolerance, freedom and the love that is supposed to prevail in the religion of Jesus Christ. The more certain one is that his convictions are true, the more he is willing to trust them to competition. Only weak, uncertain ideas need protection; truth has in it the quality of survival. This may not be affirmed in a world where iron bars, guns and pyres can stop mouths and quench dissent. But in the Christian church one should be able to have confidence that truth will win in time.

There are disputes that seem unreal. If you dig under to the roots ideas will be discovered intertwined. The interesting if puzzling fact is that equally good Christians have diametrically opposite ideas. Here is the narrowest kind of fundamentalist who is the soul of integrity, has a heart full of love and gives himself to the service of God and fellowman. Here is the liberal entertaining ideas that horrify the fundamentalist, with equal integrity, equal love, equal service. When we base our fellowship upon ideological considerations we are far apart. If we can base it upon character, worship, service we are close together.

All of this has significance for programmes of ecumenicity. There are two essentials for successful approach toward the goal. The first is the realization that all differences of opinion are not utterly irreconcilable and there is reason to hope that in the process of time there may be practical solutions. The second is that any plan for a united church must erase absolutely any rule for conformity beyond the simple requirements for working together. Our mistakes are patent. We try to agree upon a creed. We can't. Why should we try? Any statement of belief that would be generally accepted would be so emasculated as to have little meaning or would be subject to such a variety of interpretations as to nullify its apparent affirmations. Creedal churches during recent years have suffered in the estimate of their sincerity by the general public that does not take to subtle niceties of distinction, but wants words to mean what they say. Scientific knowledge and scholarly research have compelled many honest and true Christians to revise their theologies. The historic creeds do not mean for them what they meant for their forefathers. But however changed their views in conformity to the compulsions of modern knowledge, churchmen have been reluctant to repudiate the established creeds. They believe there is value in retaining expressions of belief that were woven into the history of their church. The necessity, then, was laid upon them to reinterpret the articles of faith to mean something they were not intended to mean originally. This practice is defended as a necessity of progress. The same kind of process has been at work in the interpretation of our federal constitution. It would require amazing credulity to believe that the makers of the Constitution of the United States meant to write into the constitution the interpretations made by the Supreme Court of the United States. Only a small section of our population is aware of these changes produced by time in federal law, and they for the most part shrug their shoulders and talk of the necessary elasticity of such a document. In matters of religion it is not quite the same. Religion is supposed to have a permanence, a finality that is not expected in purely human affairs. When any segment of the unchurched public is informed of the process of changed interpretation applied to creeds there is not the shrugging of the shoulders and the admission of inevitability. Instead there may be doubts and even imputations of insincerity. It would seem imperative to abandon all attempts to draw together upon a creedal basis. Either the creed discredits itself by not meaning what it says or it becomes a caldron of dissension stirred by many until its odor becomes little less than a stench.

It is equally clear that there can be no unity on a basis of organization that would imply the acceptance of ecclesiastical or theological beliefs that many find abhorrent. This procedure is conspicuously illustrated by the Roman Catholic church that never varies its reiteration that the sects must return to what it considers the one church. There is further illustration in a too frequently expressed Anglican position that combines extreme solicitude that churches shall unite with an equally uncompromising insistence upon the acceptance of Anglican ecclesiastical teaching as the prerequisite for church union. At the other extreme Southern Baptists in general and some Northern Baptists affirm that the Baptist is the true New Testament church. They even object, because of a rigid ecclesiastical concept of the independence of the local church, to any association with such an organization as the National Council of Churches. They are not amenable to any suggestion of union unless all are willing to be Baptists according to the Southern Baptist definition of what it is to be a Baptist. The Lutherans who have difficulty in uniting various Lutheran bodies are not, in general, hopeful prospects. Lutheran churches have been known to refuse to co-operate with other evangelical churches in a public service if that were to be held in a church of another denomination. It is not a cause for wonderment that even those who have liberal tendencies look askance upon many of the invitations to get together. They may be a little suspicious of those who give the invitation. The canary cannot be blamed for being suspicious of the cat that wants to get together with the bird even though the cat purrs most innocently and invitingly. Too many of our schemes for unity have this fatal defect. They must be abandoned. They will never succeed.

There are two opposing ideas of the revelation of truth. The one is that truth is revealed perfectly and completely once for all through for example, an infallible church or an

178

infallible book. We have noted that the conception refutes itself in application. Those who hold such a fundamental premise cannot agree among themselves. The history of the Roman Catholic church is one of divided councils, schisms. The expedient of sealing papal utterance ex cathedra with the signet of divine finality is evidence of uneasiness about what is to be accepted as truth. The papacy is very hesitant about exercising its prerogative of infallibility. The ordinary method in Roman Catholicism is to compel obedience to questionable decisions of the hierarchy through discipline. The parish priest must obey his bishop. He may have his own doubts and reservations. In Boston in the year 1949 a bishop silenced a priest who upheld three young teachers in their protest against what the university authorities promulgated as the doctrine of the church. The priest and the teachers insisted that this purported teaching of the church was not the true church doctrine. Discipline is enforced, but nobody familiar with history would affirm that ecclesiastical pronouncements were always consistent with each other. We have also marked the divisions among fundamentalists believing in the infallibility of the Scriptures. Obviously there can be no unity as fundamentalists delude themselves into thinking there would be if all Christians accepted the Bible as verbally inspired. It is not theoretical, it is spread before the eyes of every beholder. There are Baptists, Presbyterians, Disciples, Lutherans, Nazarenes who are devoted to the doctrine of an inerrant Bible who have not merged as one body. They are so far from it that the liberals in those churches—that is those that contain liberals—are more in the mood for union than those who profess accord upon what they regard to be the one basis of union. There are bitter disputes and vehement disagreements about what the infallible book really means.

The other view of truth should make men humble and less sure of themselves. It does not always do so for there are those who call themselves "liberals" who are opinionated and arrogant. But the nature of their view tends to moderate that disposition. The source of authority, according to this belief, is in the Spirit of God and is revealed to men according to their spiritual sensitiveness. It is like light shining through colored windows. They are translucent rather than transparent. Perception of truth is conditioned by environment, mental outlook and the receptiveness of the individual. No individual conceives of himself as the sole repository of spiritual gifts. Others who differ from him may be right at least in part. He recognizes their spiritual equality or even superiority. Who is he to be intolerant insisting upon the truth of his revelation as against that of others? There is room in this view for differences of opinions. Conservatives who have strong convictions, but hesitate to condemn to outer darkness those who disagree with them will find not only a place for themselves, but an opportunity for presenting their own beliefs. There can be no demand of surrender of convictions.

The only feasible condition for any sort of church unity is a policy—or principle—of inclusiveness. Conservatives and liberals, those who value forms highly and those who disdain them may worship together and work together even though they divide into groups that may continue different one from another. In a certain part of a town an Episcopal service may be maintained: in another part even those so far apart from ritual as Friends might invite those who prefer their simple worship to meet with them and continue their kind of meeting. In the same way there could be differences in theological beliefs. If plans for union could substitute comprehensiveness for compromise their consummation would be accelerated.

In our modern world of complex law and of organization there is apparently no escape from compromise in respect of church government. A church in which government was

180

divided among bishops, presbyteries and congregations—to mention the three most conspicuous forms of organization—would begin and end in chaos. It has already been urged in this chapter that these differences do not seem irreconcilable. All of these forms of organization partake somewhat of expediency. The exigencies of our civilization and the relation of the church to it must be determinant.

Even to the most zealous and sanguine the prospects of ecumenicity although with the restrictions—or is it lack of restrictions?—advocated here are remote. The best approximation in the foreseeable future is in the still looser association of federation. This could involve the amalgamation of missionary boards. At least for a time a complete merger might be inexpedient. In the cabinet in Washington there is now a Secretary of Defense whose supervision and authority extend over all the armed forces. But subordinate to him there are three secretaries representing the three divisions of the armed forces—Army, Navy, Air. The analogy could be helpful in missionary organizations. Denominational divisions with their respective secretaries could be co-ordinated by the secretary in chief who would represent not one church but all the churches.

There would be psychological value in one name embracing all the federated churches. This would not necessarily mean that denominational names would be extinct. Whatever the name—Church of God, Church of Jesus Christ, the Christian Church—it could be the inclusive name even if denominational names continued as sub-divisions. In a city the signs of all churches would carry the title decided upon; underneath and parenthetically the designation of the particular type of church represented as: Church of God (Episcopal), Church of God (Congregational) and so on. Yielding to necessity the denominations and denominational names would be preserved, but the unity would not be fictitious if the various denominational boards could actually effect the kind of unity described. Government, creedal pronouncements, forms of worship would continue to be within the provinces of the co-operating churches. Co-operation and fellowship promoted by such an organization as the National Council of Churches would leave denominational independence intact.

A meeting in Cincinnati in January 1951 of representatives of several Protestant churches to consider union was unable to reach an agreement. There was also a division of opinion concerning the merits of a more comprehensive federation retaining denominational distinctions as subsidiary to the united church over the plan for a small but genuine union.

A factual survey not colored by wishful thinking tends to sober, restrained hopefulness. These facts show that there is in actual present existence a movement toward closer alliance among churches of various denominations. The World Council of Churches is the crowning expression of this movement. Back of it there are both earnest desire for the achievement of unity and a vision of the glory that would beautify such a reality. Certain denominations not too alien to one another have really merged. Certain mergers may be counted upon in the near future. Congregationalists and Christians, Baptists and Disciples, even Episcopalians and Presbyterians have either united, have bright prospects of uniting or have made overtures toward union. Congregational-Christian is an accomplished fact. Baptist-Disciple is a probable development. Episcopal-Presbyterian is a possibility. Some have been so encouraged by these mergers that have come and those that give good promise of becoming that they already acclaim a united Church. Their hope is not warranted except within restricted limits. There it is not to be ruled out altogether, but by no means is it to be counted in altogether. Human nature is combative and stubborn. Prejudices easily become "principles" as opinions become "convictions." Disturbing questions are raised. Where is the Spirit of God in all this? Where is the Christianity of the churches? How do Christians differ from men of the world when conflicts are so bitter and unimportant differences are expanded into conscientious divisions for the perpetuation of which some are ready to become martyrs? These and many other questions are upsetting in their implications. We may make what explanation we can and formulate what apologies we are able but we cannot avoid the facts.

Chapter VII

THE CHURCH OF TOMORROW

The purpose of this discussion has been appraisal. But appraisal induces prophecy. In these days of confusion the prophet who ventures out of the realm of assurance concerning the firmness of a spiritual order and the inevitability of the triumph of God in some way and enters into the unexplored with definite predictions lays himself open to the charge of professing exceptional intuition or extraordinary audacity. Yet if one is not impelled to forecast he is compelled to try to relate present conditions to future attainments. One may discover trends and directions of today and consider their promise for tomorrow. Indeed one may go further and ask, "What is tomorrow?"

The conclusion to which these chapters reluctantly lead is simple, unavoidable. It is this: the church will fail. It will fail measurably to fulfill its function. It will not fail completely. That is obvious. But measured by any reasonable standard it will fail and fail badly. There is no trick of words such as so defining "church" and "function" as to produce the conclusion involved in the statement. Let us consider both "church" and "function."

Throughout these chapters the word church has been written with a small "c" and no attempt at defining the word has been made. There would assuredly be no inappropriateness in the question: What is meant by the church anyway? Is the church a definite institution with certain distinctive prerogatives and indisputable rights that connote an exclusiveness in respect of other bodies of Christians the genuineness of whose Christianity may be admitted but whose legitimacy as independent groups is denied and whose authority is at least impaired by reason of their defection from the true Church? Or is there no such entity as a church with the capitalized C, simply local assemblies of believers each of which is a church with a small c? Is there a Church or are there merely churches? Or does the truth lie somewhere between these conflicting conceptions? This issue cannot be avoided without explanation. For the purpose developed here this question is subsidiary. It belongs with other controversial matters, to the resolution of differences in the interest of ecumenicity or at least the requirements for association and co-operation of all Christian groups that have a disposition to reduce not accentuate differences.

Our approach may be pragmatic. Here are many groups of people worshiping the same God, acclaiming the same Savior, engaged in the same kind of service. We may leave the questions of theology and ecclesiology to ecumenical conferences. What is important is not to know whose institutional legitimacy may be challenged but how those whose Christianity is recognized are getting along themselves, with other groups, and in the world. Without prejudice to any of the conflicting claims to unique authority we may speak of them all as churches. The conferences in Amsterdam and Evanston were heartening not only because they presaged an attempt to bring various Christian bodies into association but because they did by their very convening recognize those bodies as Christian and promote a spirit of tolerance and a willingness to understand alien points of view. Whatever may be the eventual outcome of this experiment in respect and good will it seems almost inevitable that there will be further explorations. It may safely be predicted that there will be an increase in the spirit of tolerance and new explorations of the possibilities of more fellowship and

185

closer co-operation in America and though our survey does not go so far, in Western Europe, Asia and Africa.

This is a sufficiently broad definition of the church. Failure means not that of a segment, but of the whole. The definition of the function of the church may be formed at will. It may be the narrowest or the broadest. If the function of the church is just to bear witness to the world or against the world—witness of God's salvation or God's judgment or both it is failing and it will fail. It is not bearing such witness with effectiveness. Nor can it. It is too much divided. It is not only divided into sects, but divided in its theology, in its conception of what its mission is. It is not good enough to be a witness. It does not come with clean hands. The reasons for failure if the function of the church is defined as that of a witness will be the same as those that obtain when we consider other conceptions of the function of the church.

Consider an even narrower idea of the function of the church. There are a few who believe that it is to gather together the elect. To many this is an abhorrent conception, but abhorrent or not it spells failure. The very notion fosters un-christian complacency. Those who identify themselves as the spiritually superior condemn themselves in their definition. And there are truly spiritually superior people who are outside of all churches. To what church did Gandhi belong? It is only by denying any visible church that you can call the roll of any God-inspired company. And who of them would answer to a roll call that would imply that they considered themselves to be the select of all?

Turn to a broader, modern and more generally held conception of the function of the church. It is that of promoting the kingdom of God on earth until it shall be established in its sovereignty. This idea would include the best of the other conceptions that we have considered. Undoubtedly there would be a recognition of the necessity of a witnessing

186

church. It would also offer facilities for fellowship to all who were sincere worshippers of God and servants of the Christ. This would constitute part of its method, not to say mission. But along with the individual invitation there is a social emphasis. Its business is not just to bear witness and then shake the dust off its shoes at the threshold of a heedless world and take its departure, but to accomplish something in the world.

It is no digression but an actual part of our story to consider what Protestantism faces in America, its opportunities and responsibilities, what success it has achieved and what it may hope to achieve. To some the picture may seem roseate at first. Our purpose is to be objective and fair. And this truth must be drilled into our minds, our hearts, our consciences: neither the expectation of ultimate success nor the conviction of ultimate failure must be the determinant of our action. We must fight for right because it is right. We must espouse truth because it is truth. The true knight will not withdraw from conflict and turn away from adventure even if he knows that his efforts to snatch the holy places from the grasp of the infidel will prove vain. Drums of doom must never be allowed to drown out bugles of battle.

An acute responsibility resting upon American Protestantism is to face charitably but unflinchingly the frequently recurrent issue of the relation of church and state. Protestantism in America is virtually unanimous in its advocacy of the separation of the two. It has become an American tradition as well as an American principle written into our constitution that forbids congress to establish any church in this country. The exact wording is "Congress shall make no law respecting an establishment of religion or prohibit the free exercise thereof." What does that mean? The usual interpretation has been that church and state are strictly separate. There can be no established church supported by public funds. There is no legal barrier preventing men of various faiths or no faith at all from holding office in the United States. There can be no compulsion exercised by the government to religious profession upon the part of anyone. This conception has permeated our thinking and determined our attitudes. There is not as in some countries in Europe a religious political party. There is no Catholic party, no Protestant party, no Methodist party, no Episcopal party. There are indeed two spots of inconsistency. Church edifices are exempt from taxation. That amounts to a subsidy and strictly speaking it is illogical. The other exception does not exist in America itself, but is practiced abroad by Americans who are vehemently opposed to the application of it in their own lands. Missionary schools in the orient have accepted financial support from the governments under which they carry on their work. These exceptions do not seriously interfere with the general application of the principle of separation of state and church.

There has been a long smoldering opposition to both principle and practice upon the part of the Roman Catholic church. From time to time threatening flames have darted out. Today since the Catholic church has increased in numbers and in influence there is the threat of a conflagration that could easily consume our religious freedom. During the war ostensibly at least as a war measure the President appointed a personal representative who had the prerogatives and appearance of an ambassador to represent the country at the Vatican. The manner of the appointment was not entirely disingenuous as in a rather bumbling, fumbling fashion representatives of other religious bodies than the Catholic church were called into conference. Apparently they were either flattered or mentally coerced or more probably did not sense the significance of the appointment and did not then and there protest with the vehemence that might have given pause to those bent on this radical departure from American diplomatic practice. It is hard to believe that the Catholic hierarchy powerful if quiet in Washington had nothing to do with it. Certainly they were delighted. Later President Truman nominated an ambassador to the Vatican. The nominee eventually withdrew his name. What the settled policy will be only years will tell. Apparently encouraged by this successful assault upon principle and custom and counting not in vain upon the apathy of Protestants and their dread of seeming narrow, intolerant or bigoted the campaign for tax support for parochial schools emerged from the shadows and became both more subtle and more direct. The stealthy approach was disclosed only when Protestants were amazed to discover that in some parts of the country the tax supported public schools were already practically Catholic schools taught by nuns in the garb of their order. Another approach was along the avenue of sentiment. It had become the custom especially in rural districts to supply buses at public expense to pick up children and carry them to and from school. Catholic children were said to be left standing in the rain while the buses carrying their more favored playmates whirled by. People in general do not like to see any school children getting drenched on a rainy day or compelled to trudge a mile or two on a fair day because they are not eligible to ride in a public school bus. The same people did not realize the implications of this indirect support of parochial schools or consider that public schools with the school buses were available to Catholic children on equal terms with Protestant. There was not consideration of the fact that any religious group is at liberty to establish schools of its own, but that in refusing the free schools and setting up their own the various expenses of upkeep are likewise assumed. It was a shock to many and an appalling revelation of the trend of the times and the progress of the Catholic hierarchy in changing our fundamental law to their advantage

189

when the Supreme Court of the United States over vigorous dissent and by the margin of one vote affirmed the constitutionality of the local law that extended the use of school buses to children who were attending denominational schools in preference to the public schools.

Because of the generally admitted need for the inclusion of religious instruction in education a scheme was evolved by which an hour a week was set aside for such teaching of the public school children. Sometimes teachers from the churches actually invaded school buildings at the hour designated and taught lessons in religion to pupils whose parents elected to have them attend such classes; sometimes pupils were dismissed for the hour and went to churches of their choice to receive instruction. The legality of this procedure was eventually tested in the courts and reached the Supreme Court of the United States. In its decision the court ruled against the practice in these terms: "Not only are the state's tax supported schools used for the dissemination of religious doctrines, the state also affords sectarian groups an invaluable aid in that it helps to provide pupils for their religious classes through use of the state's compulsory public school machinery. This is not separation of the church and state." Later the Court upheld the New York law on released time permitting pupils to go to respective churches for religious instruction.

Few will take issue with the premise of the Catholic church that religious instruction should be a part of an educational programme. They further hold, however, that education should be a function of the Church. They do not mean by this that a church should be free to establish schools. Any church may do that now. They do mean that the schools should be state-supported. President Burns of Holy Cross College in his book "Growth and development of the Catholic School System in the United States" puts it this way: "We deny, of course, as Catholics the right of the

190

civil government to educate, for education is a function of the spiritual society, as much as preaching and the administration of the sacraments." The immediate and practical object of the present campaign of the Catholic church for tax-support of its school is probably to lift a financial burden from the Catholic church in America. The ultimate purpose is plainly to abolish the separation of state and church in favor of the Catholics. As a matter of expediency the Catholic church is in favor of religious freedom when it forms the minority group else its own existence might become precarious. There is little doubt about its position when it is the predominant group. The "Christian Century" (February 23, 1949) relates that a recent document signed by four cardinals, five arch-bishops and five bishops calls the principle of separation a "shibboleth of doctrinaire socialism."

The same periodical quoted from the Jesuit paper "La Civilita Cattolica" "The Roman Catholic church convinced through its divine prerogatives of being the only true church must defend the right to freedom for herself alone, because such a right can only be possessed by truth, never by error. As to other religions the church will certainly never draw the sword, but she will require that by legitimate means they shall not be allowed to propagate false doctrine. Consequently in a state where the majority of people are Catholic, the church will require that legal existence be denied to error, and that if religious minorities actually exist they shall have only a de facto existence without opportunity to spread their beliefs. If, however, actual circumstances . . . make the complete application of this principle impossible, then the church will require for herself all possible concessions . . .

"In some countries Catholics will be obliged to ask full religious freedom for all, resigned at being forced to cohabitate where they alone should rightfully be allowed to live. But in doing this the church does not renounce her thesis

191

. . . but merely adapts herself . . . Hence arises the great scandal among Protestants . . . We ask Protestants to understand that the Catholic church would betray her trust if she were to proclaim . . . that error can have the same right as truth . . . The church cannot blush for her own lack of tolerance as she asserts it in principle and applies it in practice."

The insidious approach to this goal is through the humanitarian and sentimental appeal for the needs of children. Should there be discrimination against Catholic children if undernourished little ones are supplied with milk by the state? Should Catholic children be left out where medical services are extended to those of school age? Obviously the answer to both questions is "No." But instead of using logic as a step there is a leap over it when the conclusion is that money should be handed to Catholic authorities. The school children of the state should receive benefits as children, not as members of a church or school.

It is contended with some truth that American Catholics do not believe that the separation of church and state in this country should be abolished. They acclaim this separation not as a matter of expediency but as a principle. This applies not to all but to many, possibly a majority, of the Catholic laity. They are not interested in the fine distinctions of theologians. They are not encouraged to bother their heads about theology. They are friendly with their Protestant neighbors and want to live in peace with them. As good Americans they have no desire to stir up religious controversy. Why then should Protestants be in a dither about some apparently remote theory in which many ordinary Catholics have little interest? All this would be reassuring were it not for one fact that unhappily is a determinant. The fact is that the government of the Catholic church is not congregational nor is there a body of delegates elected by the laity to express their convictions and opinions. No pope, cardinal, bishop or priest is chosen by the laity or its elected representatives. Authority flows from the pope through the hierarchy down to the simple priest. The priest receives his appointment—and his commands—from his bishop. The only path to freedom and self-determination is that of revolt. So Martin Luther discovered. The Catholic must obey the ecclesiastical authority or have withdrawn from him those sacramental ministrations of his church that if he is a Catholic, he believes are essential for his salvation. The alternative offered this freedom-loving American Catholic would be submission or excommunication. When we consider that the Catholic from childhood has had drilled into him the divine authority of his church how many could be counted upon to revolt when the church transmuted its principles into practice?

Protestants in their fear of being called bigots are weaving a web that will entangle them and mean their destruction when the Catholic hierarchy believes the hour is ripe to strike them. Their confidence in the triumph of Catholic liberalism consists of wisps of rainbow insubstantiality. The modern American organization for Jews, Catholics and Protestants in order to promote understanding and good feeling has its justification for Protestants in the Christian duty to love one's neighbors. But as the majority group they may easily become dupes of Jews who would exploit it for their own benefit and the advancement of Zionism and more importantly of the Catholic hierarchy into whose hands they play. Suspicions are lulled and alertness is relaxed. Since it is hard to squash entirely the independence of thoughtful men it is probably true that there are liberal priests who are quite sincere and hold the principle of good neighborliness and toleration. But the Catholic church in America is working assiduously to become the controlling and eventually the majority group. Should it succeed and clamp down upon the relatively few liberal members of its clergy they would submit or withdraw from the church. How many would rebel? It is folly for Protestants to try to evade the issue. The worst of it is that a solution seems impossible for the reason that intolerance is a principle not a policy of the Roman Catholic Church. It has never practiced tolerance except as an expedient. The colony of Maryland offered frequently as the prize exhibit of Catholic tolerance was nothing of the kind, as we have already seen. The argument is a hoax. There is no pretense whatever in the Catholic writers quoted. According to this principle of the Catholic church as noted in the quotations given above error and falsehood have no right in the world. Since the Catholic church arrogates to itself the definition of error and insists that the church of Rome alone is the custodian of truth a premise has been assumed upon which no doctrine of tolerance can be built. To admit liberty of conscience would make the Catholic church Protestant. The sole hope is that Protestants will remain a majority. A modern upheaval in the Roman church similar to the revolt led by Martin Luther lies only in the horoscope of the starry-minded.

It is reported that Catholic scholars are at work studying the doctrines of the church to discover if there is a way of reconciling the Catholic position with the concepts of a democracy. In medieval times when doctrine was formed and practice became grooved there was no democratic nation in the modern sense. Can there not, therefore, be an adaptation to changed conditions? It is quite possible that a way may be found or made to restate Catholic teaching so as to make it more palatable for American consumption. There may be an affirmation of the acceptance of toleration or even liberty in the United States. There is reason for suspicion that such an apparent change is an opiate to be administered to Protestants eager to believe that they need have no anxiety about Catholic pretensions. There may easily be an adjustment that would prove satisfactorily workable for the present, but should Catholics succeed in their announced purpose of making America Catholic would they continue their policy of toleration? All history answers in the negative. In every state where that Church has gained control it has not only demanded control of marriage and education but the strict regulation, invariably suppressive, of all other churches. Roman Catholicism may yield to expediency, but it requires an imagination that has loosed itself from every factual mooring to fly complacently in the atmosphere of illusion to envisage such a voluntary rejection of fundamental principles.

A more immediate threat to Protestants as well as Catholics is that of communism. While Catholicism has the virtue of sincere allegiance to integrity at its core, communism is utterly unscrupulous. Its devotees will make promises that they have no intention of keeping. When there is a cynical discarding of truth and when those who hold their word binding are laughed at as fools there seems no basis for co-operation. Without trust neither men nor nations can survive. We should be shoved back into the jungle. The communism of Karl Marx and of Soviet Russia is thoroughly anti-religious. If religion is tolerated temporarily it is only as its institutions are subservient to the state. There is, however, one whiff of hope blowing from the frightful communist brew. The orthodoxy of today may not be the orthodoxy of tomorrow. A distinction must be made between philosophical communism and practical communism. In Russia we have to be sure philosophical communism in practice. But communism itself does not depend upon the materialistic economics of Marx. If by some miracle the Soviet government became Christian it would not necessarily abandon communism. A communism more genuinely communist than the totalitarian brand in Russia could put forth its claims in the forum of the nations as a system superior not because it denied religion but because it argued that it was

195

more Christian. Or it is conceivable that Russia would conclude that permanent policy of "live and let live" would be of more benefit to the communist states and that a reliance upon peaceful means even with the risk of failure would conserve the values of a communist society best. A small dose of wisdom should teach even unprincipled statesmen that war is ruinous to the victors almost as much as to the vanquished. Communism remains an enigma and also a menace.

Over against the dual antagonism between Russia and the United States and Russia and Christian churches there may be set the amity expressed in the organization of the United Nations. The alluring spectacle is like a star scarcely discernible for the clouds. But is there really a star steadfast in the heavens momentarily obscured by clouds that are impermanent? Or is it an optical illusion? Is there really no hope? Such are the questions that agitate those who gaze out into this night of the nations. The United Nations might become the answer to all the irenic prayers of all the ages. The prospect of the destruction of all the material and with them many of the spiritual values of life is so alarming that every instinct of self-preservation combined with every purpose of altruism is crying out for a way of escape. In these scientific days when all neighbors are near and the alternative seems to be friendly union or destruction, survival obviously means some world organization. The Korean conflict was discouraging and encouraging—discouraging that even limited war should occur; encouraging that, in theory at least, it should have been waged by the United Nations together. But there may be destruction instead of survival. The almost unanimous and enthusiastic support of the United Nations by the churches has been an irrepressible expression of the tenets of the Christian religion. It is hard to see how one could accept the teachings of Jesus with their demolition of race and national barriers by love and not believe in the principle, at least, exemplified in this internationalism. But the churches must believe in it for their own preservation. From their point of view all that can be expected from a healthily functioning United Nations is the chance for survival and a means of extending international understanding and good will. These are important. But the Protestant churches of America cannot receive much from an organization that cannot even formulate a common prayer because there are so many religious differences and tensions, contained in it. Mohammedans, Buddhists, Hindus, atheists, sit beside Christians: Roman, Greek, Protestant. But in investigating the possibilities of tomorrow we cannot pass by so potentially a mighty force for making new channels for history.

One of the charges of Russia against America is that our economic system fosters injustice. We writhe under such accusations because they contain enough truth to make them sting. The perfect state has not been devised even on paper. We ruefully expect injustices unless human nature is transformed. But this does not excuse the church from doing whatever it can to rectify wrongs and to establish a more equitable order. Two difficulties should be recognized. The one is mental; the other is moral. The mental difficulty lies in reaching an agreement concerning a desirable economic system. There is nothing extraordinary in the spectacle of two equally earnest and honest parties fundamentally disagreeing. We may give even political parties in their inception at least, the credit for sincerity. Among the clergy there is a group of socialists who support socialism at the polls and who are convinced that the socialist party has the best solution for our economic problems. Others equally sincere believe that socialism would bring woes to outnumber and outweigh its benefits. Whatever the outcome may be it will, one may hope, be the result of thought, evaluation of experiment and decision by an enlightened democracy. In the heat from the friction produced by clashing ideas we must be careful not to place labels on our own opinions designating them as patented in heaven. People who have assumed the prerogative of speaking for God have been known to be wrong.

But there is a moral side. It is not as some suppose the adherence to some economic group, but the subordination of self-interest to the social welfare. This is about the hardest thing in the world to do. That in itself is discouraging. Yet if that which is right is seen to be more workable than that which is wrong we need not be altogether hopeless. Industrial relations present a continual conflict. Management and labor indulge in vituperation that in itself creates a gulf between employer and workman, but conditions are improving remarkably. Though there is a recognition of the justice of many of the claims of labor and a willingness to meet those claims, we scarcely consider the employing class as in the line for halos. And there are still those who if they dared would press down upon labor so as to extract the last drop of profits. The story of evasiveness and reluctance to construct safeguards in hazardous occupations is still vivid in the memories of the informed. There have been industries where the workers were doomed to early death from poisonous materials with which they were compelled to work. Nothing was done about it voluntarily. Nobody cared. Laws have remedied that condition for the most part. The window panes of industry are not all clean and transparent, but light does shine through.

On its part labor has become strong through organization. That implies leadership. Leaders sometimes because they are trusted, other times because they know the arts of manipulation have decided control over their unions. The leaders in general feel that their continuance in office depends upon their ability to secure constantly increasing benefits for their unions. Even if conditions approaching perfection were secured the leader would be tempted to secure more advantages even if unreasonable and unfair in order to justify his continuance as leader. If there has been need of a new spirit in employers it is equally true that many leaders of labor need a rebirth. Conditions of conflict and antagonism cannot go on indefinitely without wrecking the country. The conference table must be substituted for the bargaining table that we hear so much about. Our Christianity will fail terribly in America if it cannot substitute a spirit of friendly co-operation between capital and labor not only because there is a basic identity of interest in production, but because there is a common humanity uniting all. As usual there are hopeful signs and dangerous trends.

Here and there are arrows pointing the way to better things. A few years ago the Endicott-Johnson shoe factories voted against a union by a decisive majority although the unions conducted a strong campaign for their cause. The reason was that the workers trusted the good feeling of their employers and were loath to surrender benefits provided for them. To be sure there is ground for the charge of paternalism. And the conclusion that unions should be rejected in general does not follow. What does follow is that trust can displace suspicion; that a relation of friendliness pays dividends to all. The Lincoln company in Ohio has a scheme of incentives that seems to have created enthusiasm. The story of Arthur Nash has not been forgotten. He took over a clothing industry that was not prospering in spite of —or was it because of?—the exploiting of the workers. Mr. Nash was honest in his determination to apply the golden rule. He immediately raised wages and improved conditions. When his poor oppressed workers came to believe in him they responded with all that was within them. The result was that the Nash business became the largest of its kind in America.

With many experiments and adaptations good will has in process the making of moulds into which industrial procedures may be poured. The difficulty is in inducing management and labor to accept the moulds. When we recall how conditions have improved in a century and how improvement has been accelerated in the last twenty-five years we have a reasonable prospect for an era where Christian social conditions may prevail in industrial relations.

We have had a review of race relations. Now we may attempt a preview. There is no need to reemphasize Christian principles. Accepting these as our premise we are slowly but assuredly building on them. The immediate past is stimulating to our hopes. Here are our illustrations. Each one has the quality of a megaphone. Doctor Bunche went to the scene of conflict as our official conciliator between Jew and Arab and dealt with the acute situation in so statesmanlike a way that he has been acclaimed throughout America. Doctor Bunche is a negro.

The newspapers made headlines to announce in the fall of 1948 that a negro had been elected captain of the Yale football team. This was rightly hailed as a sign of advance in inter-racial adjustment although the innovation was not quite so epochal as it has been made out to be for in 1898 a colored boy was captain by election of the Amherst College baseball team. This Yale captain was invited a few months later to join one of the university's leading secret societies. By a strange coincidence it again was Amherst that preceded Yale in breaking through social barriers in race relations. The news that an Amherst fraternity had pledged a negro was broadcast through the nation in 1948. The Amherst chapter of Phi Kappa Psi was one of social eminence. Often had highly regarded plums been plucked by it from the tree of social recognition. Phi Kappa Psi fraternity was ranked high in the list of national collegiate fraternities. That such a chapter of such a fraternity should create such a precedent

200

was astounding to many. It was so astounding that a great furore was raised in the national organization which first suspended and then excluded the chapter when it refused to rescind its action. The significance of the action of the Amherst members of Phi Kappa Psi is enhanced by a ruling of the college authorities that after a stated date in the near future no fraternity whose constitution excluded members because of race could continue in Amherst.

These changes implying alteration in social relationships between races are to be supplemented by a similar yet different change in the business of professional sports. Professional baseball is a business and therefore the presumption would be that whatever would promote business would be seized eagerly. For many years it has been admitted that some of the best ball players were negroes. It would promote the proficiency of a team to have on its roll the names of these star negro players. Yet there was an unwritten law that only players of the white race were eligible for positions on teams in the controlling baseball organization. There might be and there were leagues of negro players but they were not under the law of the organized baseball organizations. To be sure it has been bruited that players with negro blood have been sneaked into the big leagues as Indians. Ostensibly at least they were not negroes. Then Mr. Branch Rickey, president of the Brooklyn Club of the National League, signed a negro lad named Robinson to a baseball contract and eventually brought him from Montreal where he had been serving his baseball apprenticeship to the Brooklyn Club. There were protests, of course, but they were unexpectedly mild. Before long other clubs followed the example of Brooklyn. Now there is a sprinkling of colored players in the major leagues. While baseball is business yet it involves a certain amount of social intermingling as the players of the team travel together, are settled in hotels for the duration of their stay in the city. It should be added that a considerable number of baseball players hail from the South where race separation is most strictly observed.

In 1952, a negro physician was elected as an officer of a New York medical society. It was reported about the same time that Groton School, a school with a reputation for exclusiveness, was about to admit a negro. Gunmar Myrdal, a Swedish sociologist, who has made a study of the negro problem in America wrote in May 1952 that during the last ten years there has been "a dramatic movement upward in the entire plane of living of the negro people in America." He marked the sudden change in "the situation of relative stagnation of the negro's status that had endured since the end of the reconstruction period following the Civil War."

We have considered the question of international relations and have found some possibilities of an answer that will bring peace. We may be discerning the faint light that precedes the dawn or we may be deceived by phantom lights. We soberly recognize the necessity of getting an equation that will mean peace or else we are doomed. The conflict in Korea though discouraging is not proof that the folly of a great war may not be avoided. We have inquired about the future in industrial relations and have concluded that there is a fair chance of developing such improvement that we may enter a world where the quarreling voices will be subdued—we can scarcely hope for complete silence— and the nation will not be disrupted by class antagonism. Our examination of race relations had led to encouraging conclusions. But do all these add up to the progress that idealists eagerly desire?

One of the interesting observations of human conduct is the fatuity of the recurrent expectation that if the immediate problem is solved we shall enter into paradise. It is admitted that there will be other question-marks lifting their serpent-like heads threatening to strike us, but if we cannot club or charm them into submission we can at least control them. This idealistic enthusiasm persists in face of the obvious truth that history consists of one issue after another each one appearing about as serious to its contemporary world as did its predecessor. If any illustration as proof is needed even the most cursory glance at American history will yield it. No sooner were the thirteen colonies that transformed themselves eventually into the thirteen original states free from their allegiance to England than a decision upon which depended the future of North America must be made. The adoption of the Constitution became the decision but it was reached only after a most acrimonious debate and desperate opposition. When by a series of compromises the constitution was adopted it would seem that nationalism was a determined fact. Yet the Virginia and Kentucky resolutions, the Northern Confederacy, the Hartford Convention, the sectional tension that culminated in civil war are evidence enough that the adoption of the constitution did not establish nationalism in this country. Along with this issue that assumed one phase after another, other questions appeared successively the answers to which were vital to the continuance of the republic. In George Washington's time Genet as the emissary of France supported by a considerable party in this country tried to make the country practically an appendage of France. No sooner was Genet put in his place than disputes with England became acute. Jay's treaty brought a respite only to be followed by still greater tension that resulted in war. One might continue indefinitely. To modernize we may recall that from the beginning of our history the institution of slavery unleashed controversy that became more bitter with the passing of measures to alleviate the disagreement. The Missouri Compromise, the Compromise of 1850, the Kansas-Nebraska Act were in turn supposed to give ultimate answers. None of them did. Even after slavery was abolished after four years

of intestinal war the old issue sprang up in the new form
of race relations. The abolitionists followed by the radical
Republicans of the reconstruction period supposed that
through emancipation and enfranchisement of the former
slaves there was a permanent solution to the problem of the
black man. How absurd it all seems now! Our present situation continues the story of menacing contentions. In 1914
we were compelled to fight a war that in the words of President Wilson the world might be made safe for democracy.
The Allies won. A sigh of relief. Democracy now was safe.
Almost immediately a second and worse threat took form
in Germany and democracy again was imperilled. A second
war more terrible than the first was fought and again victory
perched on the banners of the democratic nations—and
Russia. The name of that country was slurred over. After
all, although Russian communism was in fundamental disagreement with western democracy the world was big
enough for both. And was not Russia willing to join in
forming the United Nations? Now the drums of war could
be discarded in favor of the mellifluous pipes of peace.
Everyone knows how this delightful dream turned into a
nightmare.

Proof of the thoroughness of this change in political
climate was the appointment by President Eisenhower of a
negro to a sub-cabinet position. It is the highest position in
government to which a negro has ever been appointed.
Negroes have been judges in the lower courts in various
places, but in 1955 a negro was named to the Supreme
Court in the State of New York. In that State the Supreme
Court is subordinate only to the Court of Appeals. In 1955
Princeton appointed a negro to its faculty. However, he had
previously been a teacher at New York University. In the
summer of the same year a negro was called to the pastorate
of a white church in Connecticut.

The crowding of negroes into Harlem (New York City)

has produced a great deal of juvenile crime. But this is by no means confined to the negroes. White boys throughout the city have contributed their share toward the creation of one of the most serious problems of the times. The term juvenile delinquency means thuggery, theft and murder. Rival gangs fight out their differences and they use weapons that kill. The failure of home, school, church to cope with this condition is not only lamentable, but alarming. Of course this situation is not confined to New York City.

Undeniably a finger is pointed in America to a new era in race relations and no cracks on the knuckles will lower that finger.

Such is the human story. Yet there is the continued advertisement of nostrums not as palliatives but cures. The really fundamental question emerges: In view of all these incontrovertible facts has there been progress? Can we believe in substantial progress in days to come?

As usual the kind of answer often depends upon the philosophical bent of the reporter. One who is committed to a theory of inevitable progress by which eventually the kingdom of God will ascend from the earth will enumerate the reasons for his sanguine prophecies. One who believes that the world is hopelessly and helplessly sliding to destruction will present evidence that seems to him unanswerable to prove his thesis. It is a superhuman task to beguile or wrench either from his predetermined conclusion. It *is* a predetermined conclusion. The rare observer who frees himself reasonably well from prepossessions and makes an honest attempt to deduce his conclusions from the facts rather than impose them on the facts will be chary of dogmatic expressions of opinion.

Undoubtedly there has been progress. It is sufficient to cite the most obvious examples. One is the abolition of human slavery. Whatever inhumanity exists in the world and there is no dearth of it—men and women are no longer placed upon an auction block to be sold to the highest bidder. Slavery is an institution no longer justified by civilized nations. Nor can there be any denial of the favorable change in the status of women. If we confine ourselves to Protestant churches it can scarcely be denied that the growth of the spirit of toleration is on the credit side. Quakers, Baptists, Catholics do not have to flee from any Massachusetts at the behest of intolerant churchmen. The purposeful application of religion to society with the growing uneasiness at injustice is another mark of progress. A long catalogue could be appended to support the claims of those who insist that world and church are growing constantly and consistently better. But if we turn to the other rostrum in the forum and listen to the prophet whose most cherished possession is a pair of glasses inherited from Cassandra we may remark that his tale of gloom is not without factual support. We will point to international hatreds and falsifications in countries theoretically Christian for centuries. Not only have the nations failed to abolish war but possessing weapons of incredible destructiveness they are willing to wipe out civilization rather than modify their policies of aggrandizement. He will mark the infidelity in intellectual society. He will emphasize the religious deterioration in our colleges. He will recite statistics of crime—statistics that will make us squirm. He will mourn over the decay of the ideals of the family as evidenced not only in rates of divorce but in the condoning attitude of society in respect of it. He will cite the incredible enormity of the problem of juvenile delinquency as it is called. And alas! the incredible corruption in public office.

It is not possible to deny the allegations of optimists or pessimists. The plain fact is that there has been progress of which we may be justly proud and there has been deterioration of which we are inescapably ashamed. In some areas we are better; in other areas we are worse; in still others there has been little change. Hazardous hopes make only an uncertain future. Timid fears need not predetermine the centuries that are to come.

But there are fundamental reasons that convince one of the failure of the church notwithstanding the wholesomeness of its influence upon social institutions. The church holds no promise in itself of the increasing virtue which alone is the source of power. The churches will not—can not—unite. Crevices of differences have become crevasses of danger. The recent formation of the National Council of Christian Churches has been hailed with deserved enthusiasm, but as usual with more enthusiasm than was warranted. It is really a merger of co-operative agencies to enable American Protestantism chiefly to unify and organize its work for more effective service. The subdivisions of the Council if they do not become cumbersome by reason of their complexity will enable the churches together to cover an astonishingly large area of religious and social life. Evangelism, education, social activities, relations with the government and missionary co-operation are all included in its comprehensive service. It may be characterized by adjectives of the comparative degree, but not by superlatives. A great denomination—the Southern Baptists—is on the outside. Possibly, although there are few signs of it now, that church may change its mind and co-operate. But the fundamentalist groups are bitterly hostile. And even if the National Council of the Churches of Christ in America may be regarded as a step toward denominational merger such a union if ever effected would leave a terribly divided Christendom even if we confine ourselves to America. Our study of ecumenicity has revealed three huge groups. Two of them are irrevocably committed to continued separation from the third and from each other. How can a church with such divisions have more than limited success?

But that is not the worst. The people of the churches,

exhibiting many of them certain praiseworthy and Christian qualities, have no least disposition to give themselves with the requisite intensity to the principles of the kingdom of God so as to cause any really appreciable progress toward that goal. The comedies of the old Greek Aristophanes have not lost their satirical sting as a lash for society today. In many respects human society has shown little change. The novels of Hemingway and Faulkner have received wide acclaim. What sort of life do they disclose? One of sordidness and sensuality. The plain truth is that even the average decent man today wants to get for himself as many of the material comforts and luxuries of life as he can possibly acquire. He is not without his code, but the high ideals of the kingdom of God had better not stand in his way.

The unglossed evidence is convincing that Jesus did not expect His cause to succeed in this world even though He prayed as He must to be true to His principles, "Thy kingdom come on earth." Did He not ask if the returning Son of Man would find faith on the earth? There is no escape from His apocalyptic vision and His cataclysmic predictions.* Explain as you may you cannot explain them away. Apparently He did foresee progress. We have given a generous report of it. It is to be hoped there may be further progress. But the view of Jesus was essentially other-worldly. This does not at all mean that this world is to be dismissed from thought as an area for action. This world has a direct

---

* It has been objected that the apocalyptic teaching of Jesus contemplated the direct intervention of God and not physical destruction of the world through natural means. But how long since has God been divorced from natural law? Besides the objection is based on too literalistic an interpretation. Jesus used the language of His time. It would appear that the essential meaning of what He said was that He foresaw no prospect of gradual development into the ideals of the kingdom of God, but that the world was on its way to catastrophe and only through or after cataclysm would the divine kingdom be realized.

relation to the world beyond. Effort is not futile. Seeds sown here may have eternal fruitage. There appears to be something exceedingly practical for this present order and preparatory for the ensuing order. The brief tenure of the individual earthly life itself points onward for spiritual consummation. The attempts to transfer the goals of achievement to this earth can have no root in reality. It is conceivable that with his new weapons man in irrational rage may destroy himself. It may be argued that it is even probable that he will annihilate the civilization that the millenniums have been building and that the loss will be irreparable. But even if humanity turns from such egregious folly what is the ultimate toward which the prophets of optimism have lifted their eyes? An eternal kingdom of God cannot be built here because this earth is not eternal. It would prove to be the anti-climax of the ages if such a kingdom as our social prophets have predicted should be hurled to ruin in the eventual—regardless of how distant —ultimate end of our world. And what could be the purpose of such a golden age where life would be most alluring if generation after generation were to be wrenched from its loveliness by inevitable mortality?

This untenable conception of the kingdom of God has created an optimism that disregards facts and cripples the power of taking an objective view of the realities. Our faith neither compels nor permits this view that the church will so grow in grace that its influence will spread like a vine until it covers the world. The Old Testament prophets may have envisaged a universal earthly kingdom of God. Jesus never did. Unwarranted inferences if not dubious interpretations of the parables of the leaven and the mustard seed cannot stand against the apocalyptic explicitness of His teaching.

The church, however, could be expected to give a demonstration of its own life, of the kingdom of God and to apply its teachings in all areas of life and to extend its principles. The Spirit of God could not have scope for work through the responsiveness of any sizable group of sincere people without making an impress upon the world. That there has been the progress that we have related is evidence of the tremendous effects of spiritual force even when confined in channels that are inadequate. But in proportion to its numbers and position there is equal evidence of the rank failure of the church. It is true that what it has done and may do has a place in God's design and the church on earth is serving some purpose just as the creation of the earth, the advent upon it of human beings and the lessons of the centuries must have some significance in God's eternal plan.

As we seek an island of assurance in the midst of changing tides, shifting erosions and deposits of the good, unpredictable tempests and unexpected calm we are propelled by grave certainties to a faith in the few. Of some we may hope, but not predict. Even our hope only flutters along the ground. When the prophets whose flaming utterances make vivid the pages of the Old Testament despaired of the unheeding multitude they turned with joyous expectation to the remnant. The light would not go out. The few would keep it burning. So it has always been. The many may occasionally get on fire, but the fire will soon burn out. The dependable are the few who may be relied upon regardless of the thermometer that registers external circumstances or the barometer that records political social or religious weather that may become fair or foul.

Whatever may be our approach to the church it is the few who are saints and soldiers in the cause of Jesus Christ. And beware of identifying the relatively few who attend church services week in and week out with the few who are the salt of the church. Some come because of habit. Some flaunt the externals of religion. Some are there because of ecclesiastical ambitions. Some are dependent upon the church for social life. Some equate regularity and activity with Christianity. Some attend to please members of their families. Church attendance is not the criterion. Even so there are few who are always there. Consider the few who support the church financially. Not all members are conscientious or generous givers. But here again we may not identify the few who give proportionately or largely from their abundance with the few of our hope. If the finances of the church could be broken down to represent motives or proportions there would be a confusing and surprising mixture. There are rich men who give from their plenty perhaps because of genuine generosity that does not necessarily indicate any consuming Christian interest. There are other men who give from a sense of duty that does not extend far beyond their contributions. Still others want to govern the church according to their personal inclinations and their crude commercialism leads them to believe in church as in business that he who pays the fiddler calls the tune—a belief too often warranted for many a church will defer to the desires of its big giver. Perchance without his money the church could not keep its doors open. So he is fawned upon. Still others have a notion that by their largess they can buy their way into heaven. There are others that give for the look of things. Somewhat modified by the financial scale these facts hold true for contributors of all brackets. It should not be difficult to understand that the thoroughly Christian giver may be in any financial bracket. He who gives because of his love for God and his fellows, because he is interested in the work of the divine kingdom is the true Christian in his giving. The huffing and puffing and wheedling to induce the congregation of the average church to contribute enough to keep it from floundering in the financial sea is a sufficient sign of the paucity of earnest givers. It is the few not the many who must carry the finances of the church.

The modern church is nothing if not active. There are

almost innumerable opportunities for service in the world today and churches conscientiously respond to them. There is, besides, a kind of ecclesiastical nervousness that makes a church feel uneasy if it is not up and doing until one wonders if Protestantism ought not to sponsor a Trappist monastery for one week of the year. There is no need to catalogue the divers forms of service to which churches have committed themselves for they may be summed up roughly, but with sufficient accuracy, as (1) Material, that is care for the properties of the church, (2) homiletic and educational or training children and youth especially in the historical and factual knowledge of Christianity, then spiritually and in the present application of Christian principles (3) social service. Social service includes everything from a party to create friendliness and supply wholesome amusement under helpful auspices to ameliorating or eradicating the trouble produced by ignorance, poverty, sickness and sin. For these purposes churches have their organizations and committees. But the responsibility is accepted by the few. The many are contented with regular or more likely irregular church attendance, nominal contributions and possibly occasional participation in some form of church service. Many of the many cannot be counted on for even occasional participation. Again it is the few who do the work and not all of them from the highest Christian motives.

We may carry our analysis a little further. The church in these days not only enlists educators, more or less capable, but it offers courses in adult education. There are courses in such subjects as Bible, missions, social service. But how many avail themselves of these educational opportunities and how many of those that do take them as seriously as so-called secular education? Protestantism has always considered the Bible its Magna Carta and accordingly has stressed the importance if not the necessity of Bible study. Consider further that disgrace of current Protestantism in America:

212

its incredible ignorance of the Bible. The minister who holds a worthy ambition that his people shall be instructed in the rudiments of Christianity as revealed in the Bible will soon be compelled to content himself with the very few who through interest and application as well as ability will gladden his soul by their responsiveness to his patient and enthusiastic instruction. Those who have the disposition to proceed to advanced studies will be fewer. To interest the many and produce Biblical education is a hopeless task.

The same unhappy conclusions must be drawn in respect of other studies. Some in the churches declaim with equal ignorance and emphasis against what they call "foreign missions." Others are not opposed—they are just listless. They have some vague notion about "the heathen" but they are ignorant of the great oriental civilizations and of the magnificent programme of the kingdom of God and the task of the church. Again it is the few who catch fire with missionary zeal and with too many of them there is more zeal than understanding.

If we turn to the appraisal of spiritual values exhibited in Christian character, disposition and action how many shall we count as thoroughly Christian? If our criteria are goodness, forgiveness, loyalty, in short, Christianity, how many will qualify? Once more the sad answer is "the few." It is the few who have been inoculated by the religion of Jesus Christ so that it has really taken. There are many mild cases—some of them very mild indeed. Judgment may be charitable. A good number of people have some sincere religion within them. Human nature is such an intricate mass of conflicting and confused ideas and emotions that only God can understand, make just allowances and pronounce judgment. But practically, we have to face the facts. It adds to the confusion to note that not all those who belong to the select company of the interested and zealous are the best examples of what Christianity really is. There are those

whose deficiency in active service is regrettable who in-
carnate the fundamental virtues of the Christian life in
spirits and attitudes far better than their more articulate
and active neighbors who profess much. After all the Christian is not to be judged by his record in running either a
hundred yards or a mile on the course marked "Christian."

The deduction from these observations is that a few, a
remnant to use the word of the prophet exists in the church
who are sincere, loyal, dependable. They possess these in-
estimable qualities: they have the spirit of their Lord, the
spirit of love that makes them incapable of meanness and
unforgiveness, they have an interest in the church and its
representation of Jesus Christ and its presentation of the
gospel, they will extend themselves in a cause to which they
are devoted. These few are the life of the church today, the
hope of the church to-morrow. Those may not be singled
out, there may even be temporary mistakes in identifying
them, but every minister knows they are there. They deserve
teaching, encouragement and responsibility. The people
of the church in general should be given all that they
can receive. There should be no niggardly service to them.
Their need is great and sometimes they will respond. But
in general absorbing little they will return less. A ministry
to them is discouraging. Some are plainly cantankerous,
selfish, unchristian in principle and spirit. Others are good
and kindly-disposed but no fire from above will kindle
more than a tepid interest in them.

The remnant is always the hope of the church. Because
of it there can never be despair.

Turning in disillusioned discouragement from the many
to the few in eager hope, what shall be done? In our time
there is almost an irresistible urge to organize and organization for this group is dangerous. Even the good are not
immune to the temptation of pride. And spiritual smugness
is the death rattle of the religious. If rigid organization of

214

the select were attempted we should soon have the fighting phalanx of the Pharisees. And they would go down to defeat. Recognition through organization of those who are told that they constitute the saving salt of the church immediately breeds a sense of spiritual superiority that is intolerable. Often have good men alarmed and disgusted at the worldliness of the church set about on a mission of reform. They have formed a group that in the beginning was earnestly seeking the betterment of Christian living. But soon and inevitably they were regarding themselves as the spiritual elite. Thus their usefulness was curtailed, their mission ended.

Yet a common interest may draw the likeminded together for some specific object. But whether or not the few are brought together in an organization they will form cells. The cells by their nature will be active for they are living and life-giving. They may penetrate where they are not expected to be able to exert influence. It cannot be denied that they will both penetrate and permeate. There is always the theoretical possibility that a whole body may tingle with life. But if not? Because of the few the light will still shine and the darkness shall never put it out.

INDEX